THE ULTIMATE FIELD GUIDE TO LANDSCAPE PHOTOGRAPHY

THE ULTIMATE
FIELD GUIDE TO
LANDSCAPE
PHOTOGRAPHY

ROBERT CAPUTO

NATIONAL GEOGRAPHIC
WASHINGTON, D.C.

CONTENTS

6   **INTRODUCTION**

8   **THE LANDSCAPE PHOTOGRAPH**
A Sense of Place
Thinking in Adjectives
Photographing New Places
Seeing and Thinking
Subjects
34   **Profile:** Raymond Gehman

42   **COMPOSITION**
Three Elements of Photography
Point of Interest
Avoid the Bull's Eye
Rule of Thirds
Foreground Elements and Depth of Field
The Sky
Leading Lines
Framing
Patterns
Scale
Negative Space
Eliminating Unwanted Elements
Panoramas
70   **Profile:** Joel Sartore

78   **USING LIGHT EFFECTIVELY**
Making the Most of What You Have
Time of Day
Mood
Seasons
Frontlighting
Sidelighting
Backlighting
Adding Light
Flash
Exposure and Bracketing
Weather
Sunset & Sunrise
Night
112   **Profile:** Bruce Dale

120   **CAMERAS & LENSES**

138   **DIGITAL STRATEGIES**

152   **USEFUL INFO**

156   **INDEX**

160   **CREDITS**

Opposite: Humans are part of the landscape, too. Preceding pages: By including her feet in the frame, the photographer adds a touch of humor.

Introduction

Good landscape photographs celebrate the glorious diversity of our planet—its serene beauty, its majesty, and even its stark severity. Every forest, desert, plain, or marsh has a character that sets it apart from all others. A good landscape photographer knows how to communicate the unique qualities of a place—how to capture the way it looks and feels. He or she makes pictures not just *of* a scene, but *about* it, too.

Landscapes are among our favorite photographic subjects. The images we make while traveling conjure memories of the places we visited. When we view our photographs later, they call to mind not just the scene, but all the senses and emotions we experienced there. The images are irreplaceable mementos of the most adventurous (that mountain we climbed) or the most languorous (that Caribbean beach) times of our lives. We hold them precious.

But good landscape photography is tricky. The three-dimensional real world is not easily converted to a flat photograph. When we stand on a mountaintop or in the midst of a rolling plain, all of our senses come into play. We see the scene, but also hear, smell, and feel it. We can even taste the crisp air or the breeze tinged with ripening wheat. Photographs contain no such luxury. The photographer must know how to intimate these other senses in the tiny bit of data captured on a sensor or a piece of film.

You will notice that I said both sensor and film; photography is in transition. Professional photographers increasingly shoot with digital cameras, though some still use film. Most of the information in this book applies to both.

Making good photographs hasn't really changed; the

differences come after you've pressed the button, differences we cover in sections on digital panoramas, gear, and post-shooting workflow.

But making good landscape photographs is primarily about looking and thinking, not about which medium you use. In this guide we will consider many different sorts of scenes and explore ways in which the elements of composition and light contribute to the making of good landscape photographs. We'll cover the what, when, and how of shooting. We'll also get insightful tips from three *National Geographic* photographers whose outstanding images have the power to evoke special landscapes from around the world.

Throughout this book, you'll be encouraged to go out and make lots and lots of pictures. Photography is like any other skill. The more you think about it and do it, the more accomplished you will become.

—*Robert Caputo*

Photographer Macduff Everton's photograph evokes the serenity of early evening on Kunming Lake near the Summer Palace in Beijing, China.

Chapter 1

The Landscape
Photograph

1 The Landscape Photograph

Curving rows of lavender form leading lines that carry our eyes to the stormy mountains in the distance.

Previous pages: Shadow and light embrace a strip of fertile land on Lanai Island, Hawaii. By contrasting bright fog and shadowed hillside, the photographer created a graphic landscape.

A SENSE OF PLACE

We've all had the experience: Driving through a beautiful landscape, you stop at every scenic overlook to make photographs sure to capture the grandeur of what you see. You get home, look at the pictures, and they look flat and boring. All the elements that enthralled you at the time are there, but not the feeling. Why?

When we look at a landscape, our eyes travel over it and selectively focus on the elements we find appealing. Our field of vision encompasses a great deal of the scene, but our eyes and brains have the ability to ignore all except the most alluring details. Lenses and sensors or film cannot do this by themselves. They need help.

Photographs are two-dimensional, so one important element—the third dimension—is automatically eliminated in our representations of the real world. And of course, when we view a scene live, all our other senses add to the effect—the sound of rustling leaves, the smell of a newly plowed field, the taste of salt air, and the feeling of a breeze are all part of the experience. To convey a sense of place, our landscape images need to evoke other senses as well as sight.

What is it about the scene that captured your attention and made you want to photograph it? Was it the distant mountaintop, the play of light on water, the color of autumn leaves, the big sky? Something in the scene spoke to you, and whatever it was should be the point of interest in the frame. Look again at the landscape in front of you. What other features could help you focus attention on that point of interest? Perhaps there's a river or road winding its way toward the mountain, an old stone wall slicing through a field, or a flaming red tree standing alone in a grove of yellow ones.

You will probably have to hike around a bit to incorporate these elements and find the right angle. A change in the viewing angle of only a few degrees to the right or left, or up or down can make a dramatic difference in the image. Only rarely are great images taken from scenic overlooks, which are usually sited for the

convenience of road builders, not photographers.

Look at how the light falls on your subject and think about where it would be earlier or later in the day. You may want to come back at a different time, or even in a different season, to get the effect you're after. The point is

Careful metering allowed the photographer to capture rippling water along the coast of New Zealand.

that you really have to see the scene before you can photograph it well. We'll talk about how to use leading lines, framing, and other compositional techniques as well as light and weather in subsequent chapters.

THINKING IN ADJECTIVES

Once you've decided what it is about the scene that appeals to you, consider the character of the place. Think of adjectives you would use to describe the place to a friend: a majestic oak tree, a desolate lighthouse, a lush garden, a wide-open prairie. Then look for ways to emphasize the appropriate adjective. Think about how the physical elements and the quality of light will help you convey the spirit of the place in a photograph.

A lighthouse, for example, will not come across as very desolate if you shoot it in bright daylight and it fills the entire frame. It might be beautiful, but there would be no sense of its physical setting. Use the ocean and the shoreline or the rocky promontory on which it stands to capture its sense of "beacon." Try to shoot it around dawn or dusk, when your film or sensor can record its light, and preferably in fog or with a stormy sea sending spray up around it. Such an image will look quite different from another image of the same lighthouse shot on a sunny afternoon and will say much more about the idea of a lighthouse. Photographs need to be both of and about a subject.

> **TIP:**
> Take time to explore. Part of the joy of landscape photography is being out in nature. Wander around and get a sense of the place. It will take time and patience to discover the best way to show what makes it unique.

PHOTOGRAPHING NEW PLACES

Research is the key to photographing new places. Visit libraries and bookstores to look at travel guides and picture books about the place. Go online to see if travel magazines have relevant stories in their archives and visit the place's tourism Web site. When you arrive, look at postcards and brochures. Talk to taxi drivers and folks who work in the hotel. Doing this will give you an idea of what the area has to offer and will save you lots of time. It's not that you want to copy images other photographers have made, but seeing how they treated a place will give you ideas of your own.

Time is the most important investment you can make in getting good landscape pictures. When you arrive in a

place you've never visited before, do all of these things and then spend time scouting—driving or hiking to different locations, finding different vantage points. Carry a compass to figure out where the sun will rise and set, and imagine how the place would look in different kinds of light. This can take some practice because you also have to look at where the light will *not* be falling. Photographing a canyon, for example, you might see that the west wall will be beautifully lit in the early morning. If the canyon is deep, however, the east wall will be in such complete shadow that your camera will be capable of rendering it only as a great black blob. Unless this is the effect you want, you'll either have to modify your composition, shoot it later in the day, or plan to return on an overcast day when both sides will be photographable.

Look at the scene through different lenses, from wide-angle to telephoto, and think about how each lens affects it. Do you want to compress the scene with a long lens, or widen it with a short one? Look for foreground and other compositional elements that might enhance the image. Make a shooting schedule of where you want to be at different times and what equipment you'll need. Predawn photo-

In Bolivia, a Chipaya woman is silhouetted by bright light at sunset as she walks home. Don't be afraid to shoot into the sun, but be sure to meter carefully and bracket.

TIP:

Visualize your photograph. Create the image in your mind the way a painter would create it on a canvas. Then think about the time, light, and composition that will translate what you see in your mind into a photograph.

graphs usually require a tripod, for example. Check the weather forecast and make alternate plans in case the weather turns lousy.

SEEING AND THINKING

The two most important elements in any kind of photography are seeing and thinking. There is usually no great rush when you are making landscape pictures, so when you hold your camera up to your eye, pause a moment. Is what you see in the little rectangle something you would like to see on a page of a magazine, in your photo album, or on your living room wall?

Imagine that you are going to show this shot to a friend who has never seen this place. Does what you see capture the look and spirit of the scene? If not, don't press the button. What would improve it—different light, a different angle? All places are photogenic. It's our job to figure out how.

Something in a scene moved you and made you want to record it. That feeling is the most important element in making good photographs. We will explore some

Blur caused by a slow shutter speed reinforces the idea of trekking through a dense forest in Indonesia. By moving at the same speed as the hiker in front, the photographer kept her reasonably sharp.

BUILDING YOUR SKILLS, TRAINING YOUR EYE

To learn how different kinds of light, different angles, and different composition can affect an image, find a place near your home that you find attractive and interesting: a garden, a statue in a park, or any other good subject for a landscape picture. Choose a place that's near enough so you can return easily and often.

Think about the place and the feeling you want your images to convey about it. Then photograph it at different times of day in different weather—at dawn, early morning, noon, late afternoon, and dusk and on sunny, cloudy, rainy, and foggy days. Shoot it in different seasons, too, to see how they affect the mood of the photographs. Experiment with different lenses and angles. When you look at your images side by side, you'll quickly see which ones work and which ones do not. Since you know what the conditions were when you made each image, you will know why. You can apply the knowledge you get from this exercise to any situation you come across.

Take time to study the work of other photographers. Painters pore over the works of the masters to hone their own skills, and we can do the same. Look at books by renowned photographers like Eliot Porter, shown above, to study their ideas and techniques. How has the photographer framed the image? What is the point of interest? What time of day and in what season was it shot? Where was the camera? Was there a little or a lot of depth of field? There is always a reason an image catches your eye, and deciphering what it is will help you become a better photographer.

Get out before sunrise and stay out after sunset—the times when the light is best. Use the harsher light of midday to scout.

It's often a good idea to get up very early so you can be on-site and ready when the first light begins to illuminate the sky. Try to plan your predawn, sunrise, and early morning locations very close to one another so you don't waste valuable time getting from one place to the next. The gorgeous light does not last very long. In early morning and late afternoon, sunlight is warmer in tone (more red) than at midday, something we'll discuss in chapter 3 under Time of Day (pages 80–83).

It's much more fruitful to spend time on one or two locations than to race around. A great shot of one place beats several mediocre ones of many.

Such an approach allows you to be creative. Once you have recorded the image you were thinking about, try something different. Climb a tree, wade out to the middle of a stream, use a flower or other object in the foreground, try another lens or a slow shutter speed. Play with the subject and your gear. Have fun. You may be surprised at the results, and you will often capture something more than what postcards show—something original and quite personal.

aesthetic and technical ways to compose and light your photographs and how to capture on film the feeling you have about different kinds of landscapes.

LANDSCAPE SUBJECTS
Flowing Water

If a river or stream flows through the landscape you are shooting, think about the character of it and how to convey that character in the image. A big, slow river looks and feels different from a fast-moving mountain stream.

The water can be the center of interest in the image, or it can serve as an element in your composition—as a diagonal or other leading line as a horizontal line, or as a shape that complements other elements in the frame.

If you're shooting a stream, decide on its most important quality—the clarity of the water or its speed as it bounds over rocks. Compose the frame in a way that accentuates the quality you have decided on, and then choose a combination of shutter speed and aperture that will further enhance it. If you want to show how crystalline the water is, use a fast shutter speed so that the water does not blur—but you also want

To shoot this scene along the coast of Dominica, the photographer used a shutter speed slow enough to blur the crashing waves but fast enough to freeze the clouds above.

enough depth of field to keep the rocks in the streambed in sharp focus. If it's speed you're trying to show, use a slower shutter speed to let the water blur in a way that conveys that.

Look carefully for reflections in the water. You can use some reflections to enhance the image—the colors of reflected autumn leaves, for instance—but others may just be distracting. You may have to move around a bit to include or eliminate them, or return when the sun is at a different angle. Use a polarizing filter to eliminate some of the reflection and increase contrast; rotate it until you have the effect you want.

There are two ways to shoot waterfalls: freeze or blur. Think about the character of the waterfall and how you want to portray it. Then determine which approach is right. Freezing the water as it spills over a fall is usually the best way to communicate the water's power, especially that of a big cascade. To freeze a waterfall you'll need a shutter speed of at least 1/250—faster if it's a raging cataract spraying water and mist. Remember that the higher the shutter speed, the wider the aperture and the less the depth of field. Ensure that everything you want to be sharp really will be. If you can't get enough depth of field, try using a wider lens and moving closer.

TIP:
Never be content with what you see in the viewfinder the first time you raise it to your eye. Move around, lie down, find a different angle.

Blurring a waterfall conveys a very different feeling from freezing it—the soft, silky white blur of streaming water feels more serene and peaceful. To blur a waterfall, you will need a shutter speed of 1/8 or so. Use a tripod or other camera stabilizer and a remote release cord or the camera's self-timer to avoid shaking the body with your finger. If you don't have a tripod with you, try resting the camera on your camera bag, a rock, or something else that is stable. You probably will not have to be concerned about depth of field at shutter speeds this slow, but be aware of any wind that might be shaking trees or bushes that are in the frame.

A slow shutter speed turns Multnomah Falls in Oregon milky white. The people on the bridge, fortunately standing still, lend scale to the scene.

Forests

Photographing forests presents a different set of challenges. First, think about the character of the forest you want to shoot and the feeling you want to convey in your image. Should it feel dark and brooding, or light and airy?

When shooting a forest, look for open areas like this one in the Cascade Range in Washington. Fallen trees make interesting textured subjects, and they leave openings in the canopy that let light in.

Are there any special features that will help express how you feel about it?

As with any photograph, find a point of interest. It might be one slightly different tree trunk, a path winding through, or a splash of color on a flowering vine. Whatever it is, compose in such a way to lead the viewer to it. Look for shafts of light penetrating the canopy or one spot on the forest floor directly lit by the sun.

Whether you are shooting toward a forest or shooting from inside it, look for patterns, lines, and other compositional elements you can use. Try both wide and telephoto lenses. A wide lens looking up at the trees will make them soar; a telephoto will compress a row of trunks. Lie down and look straight up through the branches; climb a tree to look down the path.

If you shoot with film often, you might want to experiment with different films to see which one you like best. Different types of film reproduce colors differently, and some of them do not make much distinction between close shades of green. Fuji Velvia 50, for example, does a good job of recording subtle differences in greens, but the film is not to some people's taste for other situations. To

see what works for you, try several types in the same situation and then compare the results.

If you're camping in a forest that is very humid, be careful that fungus does not invade your gear. The best defense against fungus is silica gel, which is available at many hardware and camera stores. Put your gear and the dry silica gel in an airtight and waterproof case whenever you are not using it. When the gel turns pink, it is saturated; you should dry it in an oven or in a frying pan over a fire. When the gel turns blue, it is ready for use again.

Plains and Prairies

Wide-open spaces such as plains and prairies are among the hardest landscapes of all to photograph well because often they lack an obvious point of interest. In most cases, the huge scope of the scene is one of the things you're trying to communicate. Even so, remember that viewers need something on which to focus. Look for an element peculiar to that place and use it as a point of interest that says something about the scene and imparts a sense of scale. You don't want the viewer's eyes to wander aimlessly around the frame, so use whatever might be available to lead him into the image—a winding road, a stream, or a fence line, for example.

TIP:
If you don't have a waterproof case, use sealable plastic bags to keep your equipment dry. Never put hot silica gel in them.

Like every forest, every plain has its own personality, so hunt around until you have found an angle and composition that reflect it. What is the most important feature of this particular place? Think about the sky. Do you want a lot or a little of it? A clear blue sky might best reflect the character of one plain, a brewing storm another. Remember the rule of thirds (see page 48). If the sky is important, place the horizon along the bottom third division of the frame. If it is not, put it along the upper third.

Deserts

In deserts, heat is the main enemy for both you and your gear. Before you venture into a desert, make sure you have enough water. Remember that shooting in a desert is quite different from just going for a stroll there. You will probably be carrying 15–20 pounds of gear in your camera bag and running around to get good frames. It's easy to get dehydrated without realizing it. If you shoot film,

TIP:

After you've made the image you have in mind, walk or drive closer to the subject and try again. Proximity will make the subject strike you in a different way.

try to keep it cool, or at least prevent it from getting too hot. Heat can alter the color of films and even warp lenses and cause the oil in cameras to get so thin it leaks out. Never leave your equipment or your film in a closed car in the sun. Always put them in the shade.

Deserts are often cold at night, so open all waterproof cases for the night and close them first thing in the morning—they will retain the cool air inside for quite some time. Take a cooler or Styrofoam box for your film and keep ice in it if possible. Remove any film you'll need about an hour in advance to allow it to warm up. If you are staying in one spot in a desert, you can bury film in the sand to keep it cool. Be sure to dig a deep enough hole—and don't forget where it is.

Sand and dust can get inside equipment, especially when it's windy. Both will scratch film, and sand will wreak havoc inside the focusing rings of your lenses. Protect your gear by carrying it inside your camera bag, pack, or case when you aren't using it. If it's really dusty, use plastic freezer bags. Change film out of the wind if you can. Every time you open your camera, clean the inside with a camel-hair brush or shots of air from a squeeze bulb. When you change lenses, give the rear element and the inside of the camera a few blasts, too. Clean your equipment every night with the brush and bulb. Take care when cleaning the lenses that no sand is on the tissue or cloth.

Look for ways to show the rugged nature and the beauty of deserts. In the middle of the day, find waves caused by the heat. Using a long lens to compress them, you'll get dramatic shots that really say "hot." Deserts are also great places for pictures of stars. There is no humidity, and usually no terrestrial lights to interfere, so stars seem more numerous and are unusually brilliant. Watch the way the color of the sand changes throughout the day with the angle of the sun. Think about ways to capture the characteristics of the desert. A wide shot might best portray one desert, while a close-up of one plant struggling to survive on the side of a dune might best represent another.

Think about including the sun in your photograph— it's one sure way to say hot and harsh. But shooting the sun is tricky. On a clear day, the sun is so bright that your camera's meter will tend to underexpose everything else

in the frame. Shoot in manual mode, or take a reading without the sun in the frame, depressing the shutter button halfway to hold the exposure, then reframe before you shoot. If you're shooting film, bracket a lot to make sure of getting the exposure you want. With a digital camera, check the images as you shoot. Wide-angle lenses tend to work best because the blown-out sun takes up less of the image, but they are susceptible to lens flare. The advantage of SLRs is that you can see the flare when you frame the image.

Close to his subject with a wide-angle lens, the photographer shows us great detail of a hunter in the Kalahari Desert. The approaching figures give us a sense of the desert's size.

Seacoasts

Consider these different scenes: a tranquil tropic isle with turquoise water lapping at a white, sandy beach; storm waves pounding a rocky New England shore; a densely packed vacation beach. What kind of shore are you photographing, and how can you best convey it? What time of day, what kind of weather, and what season is most appropriate for showing its character? These are the kinds of questions to ask yourself while scouting for the right vantage point and composition before shooting. Every shoreline is different in some way. Show the difference in your images.

TIP:
Never be content with what you see through the viewfinder when you first raise it to your eye. Try different angles.

Once you have thought about the character of the shore, look for elements you can use to reinforce the feeling you're after. Palm trees make a good frame for a tropical beach; a spray of water shooting over rocks adds drama to a rugged coastal scene. As in the desert, be careful about sand. If it's windy, be sure to protect your camera and lenses from blowing sand. Don't open the camera back unless you are in an area that is well sheltered.

Mountains

Hiking is always a compromise between having all the gear you want and determining the amount you want to carry. If you can drive into the mountains, or if you are on an expedition with porters or mules and aren't too concerned about weight, pack the gear in foam rubber inside a waterproof case. Most of these cases come with foam rubber inserts that you can adapt to fit your equipment. The foam rubber absorbs most of the inevitable jostles and bumps, and the case will protect your gear from dust, rain, or snow. Tie the case onto a pack frame to make it easier to carry, but keep at least one camera and lens out and handy for pictures along the way.

TIP:
Be careful of salt water, which is very corrosive. If you get salt spray on your equipment, wipe it clean as soon as you can.

If you are hiking, though, you probably want to keep your gear to a minimum. A wide-angle and a short telephoto are usually enough lenses. Even better are short (17 to 35mm) and long (80 to 200mm) zoom lenses. Keep whatever gear you use most around your neck or in a pocket for easy access. Seal the rest in plastic bags, put them in the middle of your backpack, and surround them with clothes to protect them from jolts.

If you are shooting in winter or above the snow line, try to keep your gear reasonably warm at all times. Severe cold is hard on batteries, the oil that lubricates your cameras, and film. Keep the camera inside your jacket, taking it out only to shoot. Take plenty of extra batteries—they don't last long in the cold. Remember that bare skin sticks to metal when it's really cold, so you might want to put tape over parts of your camera.

Are the mountains you're shooting rugged or worn, threatening or enchanting? What feeling do you get from them? Look for elements that will reinforce your feeling and convey it to the viewer. What composition, angle, light, and weather seem most appropriate? Look for the telling details that reflect the spirit of the mountains, too.

TIP:

Unless you absolutely have to, avoid rewinding film in severe cold. The extremely low humidity promotes static electricity that can appear on the film as lightning bolts. If you must change film, rewind it slowly to reduce the risk of static.

Fog softens the light in this panorama of bluffs in California. Diffuse light makes the peaks look mysterious and saturates the greens and browns of the earth.

Aerials

Aerial pictures are an important part of many *National Geographic* stories because they are often the best way to capture the expanse and geography of a place. Aerials put places in context and frequently let us see something familiar in a way we never have before. They can be tricky, though, because you're usually moving when you shoot them.

Think of aerial landscape pictures in the same way you think of normal ones. Be mindful of good light and com-

Aerials don't have to be sweeping vistas to be dramatic, as demonstrated in this fairly tight shot of a Minnesota forest after a snowfall. Narrowing the field makes the image more abstract and accentuates the pattern and light.

position. Compose aerials carefully, using the same techniques for the rule of thirds, leading lines, and so forth. Patterns are especially revealing from the air, whether they are the rectangles of agricultural fields or the symmetry of sand dunes.

You can make aerials from commercial airliners, though it is difficult because you must shoot through a window (usually dirty and scratched) and you have no control over where the plane flies. If you are shooting from a big plane, try to find a seat with a clean window that is forward of the wings and the exhaust from the engines. A rubber lens hood is useful because it will not transmit the vibrations of the plane and will cut out reflections in the window. Note that the windows in planes are plastic; if you shoot through them using a polarizing filter, your shots may have weird rainbow patterns.

Make aerials with a fast shutter speed, generally 1/250 or faster—how fast depends on altitude. You can get away with a slower shutter speed if you are quite high. Your best chances will be on ascent and descent, though if you are flying over some huge feature, like a mountain range, you should be able to good images from cruising altitude.

The best aerials are made from something that can fly low and at slow speeds—a single-engine plane, a helicopter, an ultralight, or even a blimp. These allow you to get just the altitude and the angle you want, and you can fly in the light you're after. The best planes are the single-engine type with an overhead wing, such as the Cessna 206. These can fly quite slowly, and most have removable doors (usually the rear passenger). Sitting in the back with the doors removed, you will have a wide view.

Don't let the charter company tell you they can't take the door off a helicopter or small plane. They can. The view will stretch before you; just mind the wing struts and wheels. Strap yourself in, keep camera straps around your neck, and put your gear on the floor in front of you. The wind is powerful, so lean into the plane to change cards, film, or lenses.

Talk with the pilot before you take off. Tell him what you want to photograph, from what angle, and at what altitude. It often helps to make a drawing to show where you want the plane to be. You should make several passes, as you only have a brief time to shoot on each one as you circle over the subject. Use a motor drive to get off as many shots as you can on each pass. In a helicopter, you can hover once you have found the perfect spot, but be aware that hovering produces a lot of vibration.

Be careful of exposure. Aerial views of landscapes can fool the meter in the camera if they are predominantly of a forest (which will make the camera overexpose), a desert (which will make it underexpose), or some other

TIP:

Work out a system of hand signals with the pilot if you are flying in a small plane. It will be too noisy to talk, and you'll need a way to indicate that you want to be higher or lower, closer or farther away.

dark or bright subject. Think about the tonal quality of the scene and adjust your exposure accordingly. You want to use low ISO ratings for fine grain and color rendition, but you need to use a shutter speed of at least 1/250—faster if you're using a telephoto. Aircraft vibrate more than you realize, and you don't want it to affect the image.

If you can't remove the door, ask if you can open or take off the window. The copilot's window is usually openable in small planes. If that fails, clean the window next to your seat inside and out before takeoff. Use a nonabrasive cloth to avoid scratching it.

The Presence of Man

We've focused on natural landscapes, but sometimes it's impossible to avoid signs of human presence. This can be a good thing. The earlier example of a farmhouse on the prairie shows how man's presence can add to an image. Man-made objects can augment an image by adding contrast. Also, roads, fences, and railroad tracks can be used as leading lines. You can incorporate a man-made object to reinforce the feeling your image conveys or to strengthen its composition. An example is Ansel Adams's "Moonrise, Hernandez, NM," in which the serenity of a monumental scene is enhanced by a small settlement.

Photographed in misty light, a small cabin seems a living feature of the Hoh Rainforest in Olympic National Park. Notice how the photographer framed the cabin with trees.

A PASSION FOR THE NATURAL WORLD

Raymond Gehman vividly remembers playing in the woods near his home in Fairfax, Virginia, a beautiful landscape of rolling hills and woods. "Some of the trees were giants, one hundred years old or more," he recalls. "When I was 12 or 13, the whole area was leveled. I was just a kid, but it really affected me. I can still smell the torn up earth, still see the piles of burning trees. I've been passionate about the natural world and what we do to it ever since."

Gehman's path to photography was set equally early. A classmate's father worked at *National Geographic* and on parents' day showed pictures of life in the Arctic. Mesmerized by the images of Inuits and polar bears brought into his classroom in suburban Washington, D.C., he also was taken by the idea that this lucky person had the job of photographing them. He pored over *Life, Look,* and other photography magazines, captivated by landscape photographers like Ansel Adams and photojournalists like Henri Cartier-Bresson.

"The books and magazines in the school library gave me a sense of the history of photography," Gehman says. "I became very interested in the idea of merging the worlds of art and photojournalism." Pursuit of that goal led Gehman to the University of Missouri School of Journalism, an internship at *National Geographic,* then three years as a photographer at the *Missoulian* in western Montana.

"That was the best learning experience possible," Gehman says. "We had a photo staff of three, so you had to do it all—shoot three assignments a day, process the film, print, do the layouts, everything. We did mostly feature stories, so I could pursue this love I had for art and journalism."

While working at the *Virginian-Pilot* in Norfolk, Virginia, Gehman got the call he'd been waiting for: *National Geographic* offered him an assignment to work on a book about America's state parks and wildlife refuges. Since then, he has specialized in making fresh images of much-photographed places and covering threats to the natural world.

"I love to get off the beaten track," he says. "Finding places with undiscovered beauty gives me a chance to create a little world as I see it, using my own technique."

A close-up of a burned Douglas fir vividly shows effects of fire in Yellowstone National Park. By using great depth of field, Gehman shows both the details and the extent of the destruction.

Like most photographers, Gehman has migrated to digital photography. "The freedom to experiment makes photography a whole new pleasure. Digital files, software, and good color printers make what used to be complicated and expensive easy and fun.

"I hope when people see the world through my eyes they get the same joy, wonder, poignancy, or loss I felt when I made the image," he says, "and that it reminds them that there's still plenty to discover—sometimes right in our own backyards."

An aerial of an island in Lake Superior reveals a quiet landscape set apart.

An egret contrasts with earthy browns in Florida's Big Cypress National Preserve.

Teepees stand out like monumental sculptures on the plains.

Chapter 2

Composition

2 Composition

The sweeping line of the railing carries us into this image of a boat making way across Alaska's Inside Passage.

Previous pages:
The extent of the pools and ponds in Australia's Israelite Bay are visible only from the air. Nature's patterns often make the boldest compositions.

THE THREE ELEMENTS OF PHOTOGRAPHY

Photography consists of three elements: the subject, the technical manipulations that record the image, and the aesthetics of composition and light. Many people find that they are drawn to a particular type of subject—landscapes, people, or wildlife, for example. The technical elements, because they are logical, are, with practice, fairly easy to learn: choice of ISO rating and lens, how to set the right combination of f-stop and shutter speed for different situations and effects, how to use fill flash, etc. Aesthetic choices are more complicated because they pertain to a way of seeing and personal preferences.

There is no wrong way to make a photograph. But it's easy to see that some photographs work much better than others. Better images are the ones in which the composition—the aesthetics—of the photograph works with the subject to provide information clearly or to evoke a sentiment.

If the goal of photography is to communicate a fact or a feeling (or both), then you want your images to do that as meaningfully as possible. When you write a sentence, there are many ways to say the same thing, but the best and most effective way communicates with your reader clearly and directly. Having a large vocabulary and knowing the rules of grammar help us express ourselves with words. In a similar way, learning about photographic composition increases your vocabulary and grammar of visual representation.

In this chapter we will explore techniques you can use to compose your photographs in a way that will make them communicate more effectively. Think of these techniques as tools you can use when you are in the field making images. These methods are not hard-and-fast rules; they are a means of expanding your visual repertoire. Great painters begin by studying the work of other painters, by working with their materials until they understand them, and by drawing from nature, whether still lifes, figures, or landscapes. Musicians start with

scales and simple tunes. After mastering these, they can move on toward their own expression. You must know the rules before you can break them. Experiment with some of the techniques discussed here, then study the results to see how they affect your image-making.

The expanse of grass reinforces the idea of shelter in this image of an old Finnish church in a copse of trees.

POINT OF INTEREST

Every photograph has a point of interest—it's whatever spoke to you, whatever made you turn your camera in a certain direction. But you have to make sure that it's clear to the viewer just what that point of interest is. We look at photographs in much the same way we read a page of text—in our culture from left to right, from top to bottom. The lines of words carry our eyes across the page. In visual representations, we don't want the viewer's eyes to roam around aimlessly within the frame. We want to find ways to guide them to the point of interest in the image. We want the viewer to focus on it just as we have focused our lens. This concept is what composition is all about.

The vast majority of photographs don't work for the simple reason that the photographer was not close enough to the subject. It's hard for a subject to have much impact if you can just barely see it in the frame. One of the primary rules of good photography is "Get closer." If you cannot move closer physically, use a longer lens. (See the reference to optical and digital zoom later in the book.) Always think about what you are trying to say with an image. If you are making a photograph of an isolated farmhouse on the prairie, it must be large enough so that people can see what it is, but it shouldn't fill so much of the frame that the viewer loses the sense of its environment and the feeling of isolation. Experiment with different lenses and locations until you have found the right balance.

TIP:
When you go to a museum or look at an art book, think about the compositional techniques used by the artists. How have they achieved their effects?

AVOID THE BULL'S-EYE

The bull's-eye composition is the second big mistake many photographers make. Avoid placing the point of interest in the center of the frame. Such images usually don't work because our eyes find them boring; they seem too static. Our eyes go directly to the center of such an image, without an interesting journey to take us there. We subconsciously perceive that there is nothing else of interest in the frame, so we move on.

We've all seen (and most of us have made) pictures of a person whose head is smack-dab in the middle of the frame, whose feet are cut off, or who is surrounded by

A STRIKING ELEMENT OF CONTRAST

I was working on an assignment about Suriname, a small country in South America. Eighty-five percent of the country is forest, and I really wanted to capture not only the vastness of the forest but the unusual beauty of it, too. In the end, I decided I would have to get up in the air for a good vantage point.

The problem with unbroken forest is that it is just that, unbroken, without any feature to focus on. Flying for hours over central Suriname, I felt I was looking down on a sea of broccoli. I was about to give up when I spied a bit of granite thrusting up through the canopy. At last, a feature of a different color and shape that would give my photograph a center of interest—something that stood out from the monotone. I included the airplane engine in the shot to give it one more element.

lots of empty space. Such pictures rarely tell us anything about the person or her environment. Our eyes find off-center subjects more pleasing and more dynamic, and we are willing to look at them longer.

When you are photographing a landscape, take some time to look through the viewfinder. See how the isolated farmhouse on the prairie looks with the building in the

TIP:
Make a viewer by cutting a rectangular hole in the middle of a piece of cardboard, and carry it with you. Look at the scene through the hole to see if it's really a picture you want.

Placing the baobab tree a third of the way into the frame lends this Australian landscape dynamism, making us feel that the tree is standing guard over the plains.

center of the frame. Then move the house to the right and to the left, and up and down. Which shot appeals to you the most? That is your picture. The following sections will help you get a feeling for different compositional techniques and how they can help you focus your image on the point of interest.

THE RULE OF THIRDS

What you will probably find when you do the exercise with the farmhouse on the prairie is that the most pleas-

ing composition places the farmhouse about a third of the way into the picture and a third of the way from the bottom or top. This placement follows the rule of thirds, a convention established long ago by painters and popular ever since. The rule is straightforward enough: Imagine that your viewfinder has lines dividing the space into three horizontal and three vertical fields of nine equal-size rectangles. To use the rule of thirds, place your subject at one of the "sweet spots" where a vertical and a horizontal line intersect. Our eyes find

TIP:
To get an idea of how effective off-center composition is, glance over a rack of fashion magazine covers. You'll notice that a model's head is usually placed in the upper right quadrant of the frame and turned slightly into it so that our eyes travel first to the face and then to the left and down. Seldom are the models placed dead center.

compositions with the subject placed according to this rule both pleasing and dynamic.

It will usually be pretty clear which one of the intersections you should use as the focus of your image because whatever else is in the frame will either strengthen or detract from the image. In the farmhouse example, look at the sky and at the prairie. If a big sky gives more of the feeling you want, put the farmhouse in the lower third of the viewfinder. If the prairie is more powerful, place the farmhouse in the top third. Deciding to place the focus to the left or right usually depends on secondary elements within the frame and whether they add or detract.

The next time you are at a museum or browsing through an art book, look for the rule of thirds. You will be surprised at how often it shows up.

FOREGROUND ELEMENTS AND DEPTH OF FIELD

Another common problem with landscape pictures is that there is often too much empty space in the foreground. The prairie surrounding the farmhouse in our example adds to the feeling of the picture, but many landscapes contain empty space that serves no purpose. Everything in your frame needs to say something about the place. If you cannot get closer to your subject to avoid empty space, think about using elements in the foreground that will make use of that space by adding depth to your two-dimensional image.

Look around for something that fits in with your idea for the photograph—flowers, a pond, a tree, a boulder, or a haystack, for example. The element can be something as simple as the scree on a mountainside or the sloping sand of a dune, as long as it says something about the landscape. Find an angle that uses this element to fill the space and to help lead the eye to the main subject—the point of interest. You may need to crouch or lie down to get the right perspective.

Wide-angle lenses are the ones most appropriate for shooting landscapes with objects in the foreground. Wide-angle lenses offer great depth of field, which is necessary to have both the foreground and your main

RAYMOND GEHMAN'S
ADVICE FROM THE FIELD

1. Wear the right clothes. While shooting, I don't want to be thinking I'm hot or cold or itchy. Stay comfortable and loose to concentrate on making good pictures.
2. Use a tripod if you need to, but don't let it encumber you. And don't be afraid to handhold at slow shutter speeds. The serendipitous effects can be wonderful.
3. Get a soft box for the little pop-up flash that most digital SLRs have. If you don't have time to fish out your strobe, these little diffusers work remarkably well.
4. Keep your camera close when you head back to camp; you never know what you'll spy along the way. Twilight is a great time for evocative, unique images.
5. Don't settle for just one location, especially if it's a well-known spot. Use detailed maps. State atlases show small roads in great detail; so do national forest and national park maps.
6. Be generous with your time and knowledge. Others will reciprocate, and there is always something to learn.
7. Stay aware of the beauty around you, and appreciate the bigger picture, not just what you see through the lens. Smell, touch, listen. All of these sensations will find their way into your art.

A band of sunlight contrasts with curving hills in this image of the Oregon desert.

Shallow depth of field and refracted light make these wildflowers both specific and abstract.

subject in focus. How much depth of field will be necessary depends upon the size of the object in the foreground and how close you are to it. If it is something quite small, like a flower, you will have to get very close for it to be readable and to fill up much of the frame. To get enough depth of field, you will probably need a very small f-stop (f/16 or f/22) and therefore a very slow shutter speed.

Use a tripod for anything under 1/60 of a second, and be sure that the wind is not blowing and causing the flower to blur. Some single-lens reflex cameras have a depth-of-field preview button. If yours has one or your lens has a depth-of-field scale, check to make sure that both the foreground and background of the shot are in focus.

Remember that the wider the lens, the greater the depth of field. It also holds true that the wider the view, the smaller the objects in the background. You don't necessarily want to be so close to a flower with such a wide lens that the mountaintop you're shooting recedes to a tiny speck. Always keep in mind what your point of interest is, and use other elements to reinforce it.

TIP:
Be careful in the placement of foreground elements. You don't want them to detract from what your photograph is really about.

THE SKY

The sky can be an important element in landscapes, either as the main subject or as something that enhances the mood you are after. As with anything else that is in the frame, you should look carefully at the sky and determine whether it warrants much space or should be minimized.

TIP:

If shafts of sunlight penetrate the clouds, be careful not to take your reading from them because they will fool the meter.

In our farmhouse on the prairie example, a big sky may reinforce the feeling of isolation. If it's a bright blue sky with a puffy white cloud or two, place the horizon along the imaginary line at the bottom third of the frame. If it is a dull, white sky, you will probably want to minimize it.

Dramatic skies enhance the mood of landscape pictures, so always be on the lookout for them. Roiling storm clouds, a shaft of sunlight piercing a dark sky, a rainbow—all of these are photographic elements you can use. Study the work of landscape photographers and painters to see how they have treated the sky, and keep those images in mind when you are in the field.

Be careful metering if you are including a lot of

This image of hay bales standing out against a threatening sky captures the idea of approaching winter.

white sky in the frame. In-camera meters are easily fooled into underexposing with so much brightness. Take a reading from a gray card or something of equivalent value, then set the exposure manually. Alternatively, if you are using an auto mode, slightly depress the shutter button to hold that exposure while you reframe. You can also use a polarizing filter to deepen the blue of the sky and increase its contrast with white clouds.

The perfect symmetry of a deserted New Mexico road not only carries us into the frame, but conveys a sense of unlimited and pleasing horizons. Think how different this image would feel at a different time of day.

LEADING LINES

As with foreground elements, leading lines are very useful for giving a three-dimensional quality to our two-dimensional images. When used properly, leading lines carry the viewers' eyes into the frame, leading them to the point of interest. Because receding lines seem to converge in two-dimensional images, a stream or road seems wider in the foreground than in the distance, and our eyes will follow it into the picture.

Nature presents all sorts of leading lines—some of the most obvious are rivers and streams, mountain or sand dune ridges, and tree lines. But also keep an eye out for man-made ones such as roads, fences, and walls. And look for the more subtle ones—compression lines in rocks, wind-carved lines in sand, erosion channels, fallen trees, and the like.

In our prairie example, perhaps there is a driveway snaking its way to the farmhouse, or a fence slicing through the wheat, or the line between a harvested field and one that is still uncut. Move around until you have found an angle that uses one of these to lead the eye to the farmhouse.

Think about depth of field when you are composing with leading lines. If the line begins at the bottom of the frame, you'll want to make sure that both it and the main subject are in focus. You may have to use a tripod if the aperture that gives you that depth of field requires a long shutter speed.

Always look for natural or man-made frames to use in your composition. They lend graphics and emphasis. Also think about depth of field. Do you want a lot, as here, or just a little?

FRAMING

Another useful technique is framing—using something in nature that frames part, or all, of your main subject.

Almost anything can serve as a frame: a branch with autumn leaves, the mouth of a cave, the hole in a rock formation.

The framing object may be in different light from your main subject, so meter carefully. Take the reading of the light falling on your subject, and think about how the frame will look. It may be that you want it to be in silhouette, but if not you may want to use fill-in flash to get some detail. It is a good idea to make several exposures in situations like this, reducing the power of the flash in thirds from full strength to a stop and a third under. Also be careful of depth of field. Some framing objects will look best if they are sharp, while others are more effective if they are out of focus. Think about how different apertures will make the scene look.

Only low light will reveal the patterns of wind ridges like these in the Jordanian desert. Look for patterns at different times of day; they will change with the light.

The framing objects should be appropriate to your subject and enhance the overall image by adding another element of the environment, either in harmony or contrast. They also help carry the viewers' eyes toward the subject, since they give an active sense of peering through a kind of window. In this respect, using framing within the image is akin to choosing the frame for a painting. Next time you go to a museum, notice how the frames look on various paintings and consider how the art would look with different frames. A Rembrandt would make a different impression if it were surrounded by a thin metal frame.

PATTERNS

Nature is full of patterns—some grand, some small and intimate. Always look for them as you explore locations for photographs. The repetition of patterns, like the rule of thirds and leading lines, makes an image more dynamic and interesting. The pattern may be columns of tree trunks, wavy lines in sand, icicles hanging from a bough, or squares of agricultural land seen from a plane.

A pattern can become the subject of the photograph, or it can reinforce the point of interest by leading our eyes to it or by framing it. If the pattern is the subject, choose a lens that accentuates the repetition. In the case of tree trunks, for example, you might use a long lens to compress them; for an aerial of fields you might choose

Previous pages:
The rule of thirds, a
leading line, and scale
imparted by the lone
figure combine for a
pleasing effect in this
vintage Farm Security
Administration photo-
graph of a Georgia
farm by Jack Delano.

a lens wide enough to show a lot of the pattern of squares. A wide-angle lens and low viewing angle can also work effectively. To photograph ridges on a sand dune, for example, try lying down with a wide-angle lens and having the ridges recede from the camera.

Look through different lenses and move around to find the view that strikes you as the most interesting. If you are shooting near a river or lake, look for the repetition of reflected trees, mountains, or other objects in the water.

Also look for the one element that interrupts a pattern: It might be one tree trunk of a different color or a protruding rock that breaks the perfect symmetry of concentric circles in the water. These reinforce the pattern by standing out from it. Remember the rule of thirds when you compose images like this—you rarely want the one different element to be in the center of the photograph.

TIP:

Since we usually look for details, it can be harder to see blocks of color or shape. Squint a bit: Details will blur and you will see things as masses.

Blocks of Shape and Color

Some patterns in a landscape are subtle. Blocks of color, either of the same hue or different ones of about equal tonal value can enhance and give depth to an image—a round, green bush in the foreground, a moss-covered boulder in the middle distance, a leafy oak in the background. The repetition of color and shapes will be pleasing and will carry the viewer's eyes into the frame.

Lines

Lines can lead the eye into the frame, and they can be graphic elements as well. Look for lines you can incorporate into the composition—subtle as well as obvious ones. A horizontal line along the base of a grove separating it from a field might be repeated by another along the crowns of the trees. What mood do you want to convey? Horizontal lines usually convey serenity. Vertical ones emphasize power, and diagonal ones imply dynamism.

USING PEOPLE AND ANIMALS FOR SCALE

When we look at landscape photographs, our minds make a series of mental adjustments based on previous experience. We've seen so many pictures of the Tetons,

the Grand Canyon, and Old Faithful, for example, that we can easily work out their size. It's much more difficult to estimate the size of unfamiliar places or features, so we often rely on some element we can quickly recognize—frequently a person or an animal—to give the photograph a sense of scale. A human figure standing next to an oak lets us know just how big the tree is, and a cow standing in a field helps us comprehend the extent of its pasture.

These figures can be used in two ways: either as foreground elements or close to the main subject. If you use them in the foreground, treat them just as you would any other element. Consider placement and depth of field. A person standing off to the side and gazing into a valley adds depth to an image as well as a sense of scale. If you are photographing a cliff, you might wait until some hikers pass along its base. To get across the impressive expanse of the cliff, back away and use a telephoto lens. Let the cliff face fill the frame, cutting it off just below the top, and include the human figures at the bottom. The cliff will seem to loom over them.

Anything of immediately recognizable size can give a sense of scale, but be sure the object fits the theme of your photograph.

Buddhist monks give scale to the sunflowers growing along a road in Thailand. Notice the leading lines of the shadows and the road.

LOOK, THEN LOOK AGAIN

In northern Kenya, I spent an afternoon trying to photograph the Magado crater, an important source of minerals for livestock. Looking down from the edge where I sat, I saw mostly dull browns and greens. But when I looked through my binoculars, the lake came alive. The binoculars, the equivalent of a 600mm lens, compressed the pools into an abstract plane of shapes and colors. People were moving around, gathering mud.

I raced down to my car, grabbed my 600mm lens, and climbed back up. Resting the lens on my camera bag to steady it, I framed the shot and waited for someone to enter. Notice how the woman is about a third of the way into the frame and walking into it—the rule of thirds. She's also important because without her, the viewer wouldn't know if the scene was the size of a sandbox or a football field.

NEGATIVE SPACE

Just because some space in the frame is empty does not mean it is wasted. The concept of negative space refers to using such emptiness to reinforce the theme of an image.

Using negative space is particularly appropriate when communicating a sense of isolation or loneliness—a lone plant in the desert or a rock jutting from the sea, for example. Think of the empty space as an object, like any other element, and then think about its placement. You want to keep the scale of it and the subject in the proper balance that reinforces your message.

ELIMINATING UNWANTED ELEMENTS

Everything you can see in the viewfinder will be part of the image and should have a reason for being there. Look carefully. If you see something that seems out of place, change your angle or location. If an item doesn't help the image, get rid of it.

The most common unwanted elements in landscape pictures are power and phone lines, poles, and distant buildings. Also look out for more subtle ones—a branch in the frame, a piece of litter. It pays to study the image in the viewfinder carefully. If you don't notice small things when you make the image, you probably will when you print. Viewers almost certainly will.

PANORAMAS—WHEN YOU NEED A LARGER VIEW

Sometimes a scene is just too sweeping to be held inside the confines of a conventional image format. A vast prairie, a mountain range, or a cityscape might cry out

The vastness of the Sahara Desert is reinforced by the use of negative space and the blending of sand and sky. Notice how the rule of thirds emphasizes the feeling.

for the space that's possible only in a panorama. Until recently, good panoramas were beyond most of us—but not anymore.

Digital photography has transformed the making of panoramic images. Before the evolution of current cameras and software, panoramic photographs required either specialized (and often expensive) equipment or laborious time in the darkroom. Panoramic film cameras, which work either with ultrawide lenses or by rotating the camera lens through an arc, record from about 140 to 360 degrees of a scene on an elongated strip of film.

Creating panoramas with an ordinary film camera requires carefully shooting overlapping images, then painstakingly assembling them into one scene while processing, or cutting and pasting, finished prints. Both of these methods still work, of course, and several companies manufacture digital panoramic cameras that make images in the same way as their film forebears. But digital imaging has revolutionized panoramic photography for those who do not wish to invest in a specialized camera. You still have to take the images that make up the panorama, but your computer, and sometimes your camera, can do everything else.

Shooting Panoramas

A good panoramic photograph is the result of careful planning and shooting of the images of which it is composed. Consistency is the keyword—consistency of perspective, exposure, and white balance.

Don't move or zoom in or out between shots. If you're shooting two images that you plan to merge, chances are that the light falling on them will be pretty much the same; if you're shooting four or five or more, it's likely that some will be in full sun, and some backlit. You want the resulting panorama to look natural, so you may have to override your camera's automatic exposure by holding the exposure lock button or shooting in manual mode. If you don't, the result may have an odd, where-the-heck-was-the-sun look.

You can shoot images for a panorama by handholding the camera, but the best results usually come from using a tripod. Make sure that the tripod is both steady and level. If you shoot a lot of panoramas, it's worth investing in a tripod that has a liquid level built in so that you can level it quickly. Before you shoot, pan through the area you plan to photograph to make sure the horizon stays level. On some tripods the camera does not sit directly over the center of rotation, so watch out for tilt.

When shooting panoramas, try to keep the whole image in mind. None of the five images are particularly striking on their own, but together they make an interesting panorama.

A good rule of thumb is to overlap successive images by 25 to 40 percent. This will give your software sufficient information to accurately merge the images later. Look for a landmark about a third of the way into the frame, then rotate your camera so the landmark is a third of the way in on the other side. (You can shoot either from left to right or right to left, or from top to bottom or bottom to top if it's a vertical panorama.) Some cameras, such as a line of models from HP include an overlay in the viewer for easy alignment from shot to shot.

Once you've made your exposures, check them in the viewer of your camera. Many cameras offer multiple-frame viewing so you can see a number of images at once. Some cameras even have in-camera stitching so you can preview and save the panoramic image as well as the individual frames.

Angle is important. Don't be afraid to crouch, lie down, or generally make a fool of yourself to get in the right position.

If your camera does not merge the frames, you can download them to your computer and use imaging software to do the same thing. Many popular software programs offer stitching functions that are usually as easy as identifying the frames you want to use and clicking your mouse. The stitching function has differ-

JOEL SARTORE'S ADVICE FROM THE FIELD

1. More photos are wrecked by a bad background than by anything else. I build my photos from the background forward.
2. The light is best early in the morning and late in the day when it's sunny, or anytime when it's overcast.
3. Be selective about what you shoot. I use the "Hey, honey" test. If I'm driving along with my wife and see something, is it interesting enough for me to interrupt whatever she is doing to point it out to her? If not, then it's probably not going to make a very good picture.
4. Take lots of bug spray, a big hat, and lots of water.
5. Camera bags are cumbersome. I wear a vest that can hold all my gear.
6. Everyone says shoes are important, and that's true. But don't forget about good socks—they'll help prevent painful blisters from all your tramping around.
7. Carry a flash cord so you can get the strobe off your camera. The angle of the light can make all the difference.
8. Try not to bore people. If your picture doesn't grab them, they won't bother to really look at it.
9. Keep shooting, even after you think you've got the picture. You'll be surprised at what else you come up with.
10. Take more bug spray.

ent names in different programs (Adobe Photoshop®, for example, calls it Photomerge), so you may have to look up "panorama" in the software's help menu to find it.

If the alignment looks a bit off after the software has worked its magic, you can tweak the panorama by dragging the individual images. If you shoot on film and scan your photographs, you can use those files to make panoramas, too.

PHOTOGRAPHING PLACES WHERE MAN AND NATURE MEET

Joel Sartore fell in love with photography while getting his journalism degree at the University of Nebraska–Lincoln. "Being in the darkroom was all I cared about," he says. "Everything else just seemed to get in the way."

Six years at the *Wichita Eagle*, as photographer and then director of photography, honed Sartore's photographic skills as well as his growing passion for telling stories about the way man's activities intersect with the natural world. This theme, and Sartore's offbeat sense of humor, have been hallmarks of his career since he began working for *National Geographic* in 1989.

"Landscapes are crucial because of the context they provide," he says, "but they are about the hardest photographs to make. Even the word 'landscape' has a sort of sleepy quality to it. Landscapes have to sing," he explains. "They have to be just as jawdropping as any other kind of picture. That's why I always try to put some juice in my pictures. We all know what a flower looks like, so I get really close to the flower with a wide-angle lens so you can see the environment the flower lives in. That gives it meaning and perspective. When there's a bee on the flower—then you've got something.

"Photographs have to take people places," Sartore continues. "Otherwise people just skip by them." Sartore believes photographs should make people care about those places, too. Reflecting his concern for the natural world, his recent *National Geographic* magazine stories include "Brazil's Wild Wet: Pantanal," "Drilling the West," and "Grizzly Bears." "What motivates me now," he says, "is showing what's at risk and how it's at risk—to show how heavy a hand man has on the land."

Sartore is well known for his stunning and evocative photographs, and for provocative juxtapositions—an enormous jet soars above a delicate butterfly, wild caribous stare at each other across a frozen tundra that recedes to an oil refinery. Humor is there, too, in the gaze of a ferret or the

Strange ship on a rolling sea of green: By waiting for late, low light, Sartore transformed the mid-western plains.

curious look of South American viscachas.

Recently, Sartore has been making photographs at twilight before the sun rises and after it sets, using fill flash to bring out details in the foreground. "We tend to want to shoot directly into the setting or rising sun," he says, "but then all you get are silhouettes. The quality of the light on the horizon opposite is often stunning, casting a lovely glow over everything.

"Think of the world as a stage," he says, "then look for perfect light. That's where the pictures are."

Strobes added light in the foreground of this image, helping capture detail and mood.

Chapter 3
Using Light Effectively

3   *Using Light Effectively*

Dusk is a wonderful time to create atmosphere. A slower shutter speed reveals the lights but freezes the Venetian gondolier.

Previous pages: Mood, like the setting sun, is reflected in this almost monochromatic image of Kunming Lake in China.

Good landscape photographs are documents of the appearance of a place and its character. You get a certain feeling when you are outdoors gazing at some aspect of nature, and your images should convey that feeling to the viewer. As mentioned earlier, think of adjectives you would use to describe the place to a friend, and how best to visually convey their meanings. The time of day and time of year you choose to make your photograph will have a great impact on how the place comes across. Would one kind of weather be better than another? Would early morning light be best? Would a different season be more appropriate?

MAKING THE MOST OF WHAT YOU HAVE

Getting the light and weather that best enhance the feeling you have about a place is the part of landscape photography that requires the most planning and patience. You may have to return to the place for several days, or even come back months later to get what you really want, but a good image is worth the effort.

There will, of course, be times when you can't go back. In this case, you have to do the best you can, using compositional and other techniques to make the best image possible in the circumstances. You can't do anything about the weather, but you can make the most of what you have.

Time of Day

The easiest way to see how light affects a scene is to look out your home or office window. As an exercise, look out in the early morning, around noon, and in late afternoon on sunny and cloudy days in all seasons. The scene will look and feel very different each time. You may want to make notes describing the look and the feeling. Better yet, make photographs every time, then lay them out next to each other and compare the feelings they evoke.

The light is warmer early and late, when the sun's rays are longer and contain more of the red end of the spec-

trum. This, to our eyes, produces a more pleasant visual palette than the whiter and harsher light of noon. The longer shadows also create modeling, giving more contour and definition to a scene. Overcast days produce a bluer light, making everything seem colder, and the lack of shadows makes objects seem flat. Similarly, you might

When the sky is full of color, make it your subject, as in this view of the Rockies.

notice how a room with warm incandescent lamps feels very different from one lit by overhead fluorescent bulbs. Light affects mood, and understanding how it does will help you make images that convey the feelings you're after.

This is not to say that you should shoot all your landscapes in the warm light of sunny early mornings and late afternoons. When to shoot depends on what you want to say about a place and how it feels to you. Some

images might call for harsh light, or you might want to use the heat waves that rise from a desert in the middle of the day. Other subjects might best be shot in the soft light of cloudy days.

Mood

Quality of light is one of the most important elements of photography. The word, after all, derives from the

Greek words for "light drawing." Light affects everything about an image, from the way a subject looks to the mood it conveys, and light is always changing. Each time of day has its own quality of light, as do various kinds of weather and different seasons. And qualities of light—of direction and color—fit different scenes and moods. When you paint a house, you choose the color that enhances the mood that you want for a particular room. You should choose just as carefully the quality of light you want for your images.

Seasons

Places look and feel very different at different times of year, and you can use seasonal qualities to reinforce the message of your landscape photographs. If you're making photographs from your home or office window, as suggested previously, notice how the same scene looks at varying times of year. You will be amazed how the mood of a scene changes, just as a person's does.

Use the light and elements of the seasons to enhance your images. If you're making a photograph of a mountain, include a field of wildflowers in the foreground to accentuate the feeling of spring. In winter, you might

When form is more important than detail, use backlight. Notice how the photographer used the beam to obscure the sun.

BRUCE DALE'S ADVICE FROM THE FIELD

1. Simplify your gear. Less is more. It's often faster to move closer or step back than to fumble with gear that encumbers you.
2. A good tripod is important for landscapes. If you're waiting for just the right light, you can be set up and ready if the camera is mounted on a tripod. It's critical when you're working with graduated filters. However, don't let the tripod dictate camera position. Choose the camera position very carefully—even an inch or two can make a difference—and then position the tripod at that spot.
3. Pay attention to times when the sun is just at the edge of the clouds. It softens the foreground in an almost imperceptible way.
4. Watch for shadows the clouds cast on a scene. They can add depth to your image.
5. To check the position of the sun and clouds, don't look directly at the sun. Check the reflection of the sun and clouds in the lens of sunglasses held in your hand.
6. If you're using a graduated filter, place the line carefully. Hide it along a natural line in the scene. Tip it if necessary. Your lens will stop down when you shoot the image—the line will be a bit sharper than it looks through the viewfinder. Don't limit yourself to using the filter only on the sky; use it upside down if there is a lot of bright light in the foreground.
7. Sunlight is nice, but give me fog or rain any day. Moody light can make for some dramatic images, and greens take on a magical quality in rainy weather.
8. Wear good shoes. (Shoulder and ankle fractures taught me this lesson.)

include a frozen stream; in autumn, trees with brilliantly colored leaves. Think about elements that express the feeling of the season you are shooting. But try to avoid clichés. Flowers obviously say "spring" and icicles say "winter." Try to find a different way of viewing these subjects—a different angle, a different lens, a different background. You want your images to reflect how they strike you and to capture what made you want to photograph them.

WORKING WITH FRONTLIGHTING

We usually make photographs of landscapes with the sun shining on them from behind us; this is the way we normally see things and the view that usually strikes us. Usually the most flattering photographic light is when the sun is at about a 45-degree angle to the subject. This is not a hard-and-fast rule, however, and you should always move to see how different angles of light affect a scene.

At an angle of 45 degrees, the sun gives modeling to the scene, casting shadows that make objects stand out in relief. If the sun is directly behind you, at 90 degrees to the subject, the landscape will look flat, devoid of contours that lend it depth. As mentioned above, the lower the sun, the longer the shadows and the warmer the light. Frontlighting also generally brings out the colors in a landscape best and allows the camera to pick up more detail.

TIP:
Gaffer's tape is an essential photographic accessory. Among its uses: taping reflectors and strobes in place, and sealing camera cases.

SIDELIGHTING

Sidelighting can create very dramatic effects, fully illuminating one side of your subject and casting the other half in deep shadow. If you are looking for shapes or patterns, sidelighting can accentuate them.

Exposure can be tricky with sidelighting. In-camera meters that average a scene will tend to underexpose the lighted side and overexpose the shadow. Take the reading from the fully lit part by getting close to it or by using a spot meter if your camera has one.

BACKLIGHTING

Don't forget to look over your shoulder in your search for good images. Backlighting can be used to create beautiful effects and bring out qualities of subjects that may be hidden when they are lit from the front. Leaves, icicles, the feathery hairs around a head of wheat—all sorts of things look gorgeous when they are backlit, and they can take on a completely different quality.

Backlighting is trickier than frontlighting because it often creates great contrast within the frame. If you are shooting a scene in backlight, look at it carefully. What part of it do you want to be properly exposed? What part do you want to see in detail? If there is a lot of sky, the brightness in it may overpower the scene and fool the meter into underexposing everything else. If the

Same image, different light: If a silhouette feels too stark, you can add detail to a foreground subject by using fill flash. Bracket the flash unit to get the light you want.

sky is an important element, that's fine; if it's not, try to compose differently to eliminate most of it. If you keep a lot of sky in the frame and expose for something on the ground that is backlit, the sky will "blow out" and be distracting.

When a subject is backlit, you usually want to see the detail in it and have the fringes a bit bright. You should meter off the subject and think about how everything else will be rendered. There are also times when you want the subject to be in silhouette. In this case, expose the background properly and photograph the subject against it. Whenever you shoot a sunrise or sunset, you are shooting a backlit scene.

WHEN YOU NEED TO ADD LIGHT

Often, subjects in the foreground of your image will be in shadow or in different light from that shining on the background. This is especially true if you are shooting in

FILL FLASH

Without flash (left), the buoys are dull. With it (right), they pop.

Working on a story on Cape Cod, I noticed a wall with vivid fishing buoys. The day was overcast and gray, making the colors muted, as in the frame at left. That's not what I wanted for this shot, so I pulled out my strobe.

An electronic flash unit pointed straight at the wall would be way too much; the flash would bounce off the whites on the buoys, creating hot spots, and would cast deep shadows on the wall behind. It would also overpower the ambient light, destroying the mood. The point of fill flash is to add just enough light to bring out colors and details, but it should be imperceptible.

To warm the light from my flash unit, I taped a piece of very light orange gel over the head. This trick makes the light from the flash match more closely the color temperature of early and late sunlight. I used a small cap of white plastic that diffuses the light and softens shadows.

Meter the scene as you normally would, set the lens aperture and shutter speed, and try different output settings on your strobe. I usually work in 1/3-stop increments, decreasing the output until I reach the minimum. Some scenes require only a tiny bit of added light. The image at right was made with the flash set at −2 stops. The colors are vivid and there is more detail in the wall behind. If you hadn't seen the other picture, you would never know light had been added.

a backlit situation, but it can also occur if a tree, canyon wall, or something else is casting a shadow. If the image you're after is one where the shape of the object—the outline of a tree, for example—is most important, then casting it in silhouette is just what you want. The graphic outline is more interesting than the tree clearly rendered. If you want detail in the tree, however, you will have to add light. Adding light also helps overcome some of the harshness of midday sunlight by softening the shadows on your subjects. If you are making an image at a less than optimal time of day, you can use a reflector or flash to get a decent image out of what might otherwise seem unphotogenic.

In general, subjects in the foreground and reasonably close are the ones you should think about. Consider how much or how little detail you want in them. Objects that are far away and rather small may not matter too much, since the viewer will not be able to see them clearly. If there's something important, you can add light to it no matter what the distance.

If you're using a reflector, set it up near the object so the light is strong enough to register. Be sure to hide it from the camera—behind a rock or other obstacle. If you're using a flash, set it up with a slave, a remote trigger that will activate the unit when the camera is fired. Be sure that the slave can "see" the transmitter or other strobe unit that will activate it, but also be sure you cannot see it in the frame. You can use multiple reflectors or slave-activated strobes to light up several objects.

Reflectors

Almost anything white will reflect light onto a subject— a piece of white cardboard or construction paper, a sheet, etc. There are also several commercial reflectors, some of which fit into small packages so they are easy to carry. Some of these have white on one side and gold (which throws a stronger light) on the other. Be aware that the light from the gold side is quite contrasty and warmer than the sunlight.

You will be able to see the effects of a reflector just by looking at the subject as you move the reflector to bounce less or more light. The closer the reflector is to the subject, the stronger the light, and whatever is most pleasing to your eye will probably be the most pleasing image. Think about what qualities you want to emphasize in the subject: Do you want to see full detail? Then you should try to make the light on the subject equal or nearly equal to that on the background. If you want the subject to be slightly darker, then bounce a little less light into it, and so on all the way down to full silhouette.

FLASH

You can also use flash units to add light to subjects within your frame, and the same principles apply as with reflectors. Think about how much or how little light you want to add to the subject, and then adjust the flash unit accordingly.

TIP:

Lens flare can be a problem with wide lenses. Use your hand or a piece of cardboard to screen the lens from the sun—but keep the screen out of the frame.

Shot from a distance, the people on the beach become an element in this seascape and tell us something about its appeal and character.

Most modern flash units incorporate features that allow you to adjust the output, often in 1/3 increments. If you make no adjustments, the flash will throw out enough light to make the subject of equal exposure value to the rest of the scene. If you want full detail, this may be right. If you want it to be slightly darker, decrease the output by 1/3, 2/3, a full stop, or even

A slow shutter speed captures the rain streaking as it falls, giving us a sense of the Honduran forest.

more, depending on the effect you want.

If your flash unit is mounted on the camera, the light will hit the subject straight on. You may want to hold the flash to one side to get a slightly less direct hit. Most flashes have cords so that they can be removed from the camera and still communicate with it. Remember that flashes have limited range. You can't use one on your camera to light up something that is far away. Move closer, or use a slave.

EXPOSURE AND BRACKETING

There is nothing worse than coming home from a shoot and seeing an image that would have been perfect if only the exposure wasn't wrong, so always think about your exposure.

Modern cameras have remarkably sophisticated metering capabilities, but even these can sometimes be fooled. When you look through the viewfinder, think about the tonal qualities of what you see. If you are shooting a beach, a snowy hill, or a scene that includes a lot of sky, your in-camera meter will tend to under-expose. If what you see is very dark, your camera will overexpose. Use a gray card like the one on the inside cover of this book or something in the scene of equal value to take your reading.

In any situation, and especially in landscape photography where you have plenty of time, it makes sense to bracket your exposures. Scenes are often very contrasty, with areas that are very bright and very dark. Bracketing ensures that you will get at least one image with the proper exposure.

The other reason to bracket is that shutters are mechanical things and are not always 100 percent accurate. You may set the shutter speed at 1/125 of a second, but chances are that the actual time of exposure is not 1/125—it may be 1/100 or 1/150. To compensate for this, you need to bracket.

The most common way to bracket is to make three images—at your reading, a half-stop under, and a half-stop over. Some cameras can even be programmed to do this automatically. If a scene presents extreme lighting challenges, bracket way up and way down. You may not be able to judge the results accurately in your camera's small viewer.

TIP:
If you are staying in one place for several days, check out the long-range weather forecast and plan your shoots around the weather that is best for specific subjects.

WEATHER

Each kind of weather has its own particular quality of light and its own mood. Think about the weather that can best convey the feeling you are after. If you want a forest to feel "brooding," for example, it would be more appropriate to shoot it on a foggy day than on a sunny one. The important thing to remember is that so-called bad weather should not keep you from getting out and shooting. It might be exactly what you need.

Sunny Days

We most often shoot landscape pictures on sunny days—they are the kind of days that lure us outdoors in the first place, and they usually both look and feel good. But there are a few things you should keep in mind, some of which we have touched on before.

The warmer quality of early morning and late afternoon light is generally the most pleasing and often makes landscapes look their best. Get out early and stay late to take advantage of the low angle of the sun. When you

scout a location, always think about how the sunlight will fall in the morning and in the afternoon and plan your shoot for the best light.

Shooting early or late is not an unbreakable rule, though. You might want to photograph certain landscapes in midday light, if the effect you want—severity or harshness—is best achieved by doing so. In this case, don't be afraid to shoot around noon. If you do, you

Cities make interesting landscapes, too, especially when fog lends them an eerie quality, as in this shot of Copenhagen. When the weather is bad, get out there.

might want to use a reflector or fill flash to add detail to a subject in the foreground. You also might want to include lens flare if it helps the overall effect. Be careful, though. If lens flare is done right, it accentuates the feeling of "hot," but if it's slightly off, it will produce fog on the image. You can check lens flare by using the depth-of-field preview button if your camera has one. Use a lens hood to reduce unwanted lens flare.

Cloudy Days

Just because the sun isn't shining, don't think you can't make great landscape pictures. There are all kinds of cloudy days, from completely socked-in dull to puffy white. Cloudy skies can enhance the mood of landscapes and evoke feelings that are not possible when it is sunny.

If the clouds in the sky are not too thick and show an interesting pattern, you can make them part of the composition of the image. If they are just a thin white sheet, though, you will probably want to compose in a way that minimizes their presence in the frame; they will appear in the photograph simply as a white mass. Be careful metering if there's a lot of white sky—it will make the in-camera meter tend to underexpose.

Thick clouds can make for beautiful landscape pictures, as the light penetrating them becomes very soft and muted, increasing color saturation. Especially for images where rich color is important, like autumn leaves, thick clouds can be a bonus. If you are shooting with low ISO, which is usually preferable because of fine grain and color rendition, be conscious of depth of field. There may not be a lot of light on very cloudy days, and you may have to use a really slow shutter speed (and a tripod) to get the depth of field you want for the image.

> **TIP:**
> Shoot a rainy scene with both fast and slow shutter speeds to see the effects of freezing and blurring.

Rain

Rain can produce some beautiful images, so don't be put off by the prospect of getting a little wet—just try to keep your gear dry. Rain adds atmosphere, especially for moody shots. First, think about how you want the rain to appear. Raindrops usually will not show up very well against a light background, so try to offset them with something dark behind. If this isn't possible, find something that makes it apparent to the viewer that it's raining—raindrops creating circles on the surface of a lake, for example.

Also look around to see how the rainfall affects the scene. Water may glisten on leaves or rock surfaces, colors of moss and other plants may be richer, and the windward side of tree trunks may be darker, adding interesting contour.

Determine whether you want the rain to be frozen in place or streaking through the image. If you want to freeze it, use a shutter speed of at least 1/125. At 1/60, the rain will record as streaks, and they'll get longer as the shutter speed gets slower. Remember to shoot the drops against something dark.

To keep your equipment dry, stand on a porch or under some sort of overhang. There are commercially made plastic covers for cameras, but you can also use a plastic bag. Wrap it around the camera, leaving one hole for the lens and one for your eye. Lens hoods are a good idea, too, but it's almost impossible to keep some rain from getting on the lens. Check and clean it frequently if necessary.

The force of a winter storm is emphasized by this strong diagonal composition of mountains in Nevada.

Fog and Mist

Another reason for getting up early when you are making landscape photographs is to be on-site in case there is fog or mist. It doesn't take long for the sun to burn it off. Fog enveloping a highland forest or mist rising slowly from a lily pond can add dimension and feeling to an image and create an air of mystery. Local people can often advise

TIP:
If you're using flash, consider the density of fog or mist. If it's moderately thick, light from the flash will bounce off the water droplets and never reach the subject, much the way car headlights light up the fog and not the road. If detail in a subject fairly near you is important, use a remote strobe set up with a slave near the subject.

you as to where and when there is likely to be mist.

Like clouds, fog and mist come in all sorts of densities. They can be white or gray, thick or thin. Be very careful metering. Think about the tonal quality of the fog. If the fog appears lighter than neutral gray, take a reading from your subject or from a gray card. Always remember that your eyes can see detail a lot better than sensors or film can, so if detail is important and the fog or mist is thick, you probably need to move closer to your subject.

Shooting in fog and mist is one situation in which it really pays to have good lenses. The better the lens, the better the light transmission and the more detail in the image. It also pays to bracket, because it takes a lot of practice to get a balanced exposure that works for both the fog and the subject.

Snow

The most frequent problem people have when making photographs in snow is underexposure. All that bright white easily fools meters—they try to make it mid-tone gray. Take a reading from your subject, or if that isn't possible, use a gray card or something else of equal tonal value, making sure that it is in the same light as

Heavy storm clouds contrast with the playfulness of a softball game in Montana. The image would be less interesting without the netting as a foreground element.

your subject. Don't be surprised if that reading is as much as two stops different from your in-camera meter. Bracket if it's an important shot.

If you are shooting a lot in the same snowy situation, you can set the exposure compensation button included on many cameras so that you don't have to go through the calculation process for every shot. Determine what the difference is between what the camera is reading and what you've found is the proper exposure. If it's a difference of one stop, set the exposure compensation control to +1, and so forth.

If you're shooting film and your camera does not have an exposure compensation control, you can accomplish the same effect by changing the ISO rating of the film. If you're using ISO 100, change it to ISO 50 so that the camera meter will give the film twice as much light. (Halving the ISO doubles the amount of light hitting the film or digital card; doubling the ISO halves the light. Each f-stop lets through twice the light of the preceding smaller f-stop.)

As with most situations, early or late is best on sunny days in the snow. The long angle of the sun gives contours to mounds, ridges, and other irregularities in the snow and casts a warmer light. Try not to shoot with the sun directly behind you—the light bouncing straight back at you from all that white will be blinding and devoid of detail.

Protect your gear from both snow and cold. If it's snowing, wrap the camera in a plastic bag as you would for rain. If it's severely cold, try to keep the camera reasonably warm so that the batteries will work efficiently and the film does not become too brittle. Film leaders can snap off, making those rolls useless. It's a good idea to keep your camera inside your outer jacket, pulling it out to make photographs and returning it when you're on the move. You don't want the camera to get too warm, though, because water will condense on it, then freeze when you pull it out.

Remember, too, that flesh will stick to very cold metal. Cover with tape the parts of the camera that you will be touching, including the place where your nose presses against the camera body. To keep condensation

Previous pages:
Luck required: You
never know where light-
ning will strike or
what it will look like.
Frame the part of land
and sky you want,
stand in a safe place,
and be patient.

from forming on the equipment when you enter a warm room, put it in a sealed plastic bag while you are still out in the cold and allow it to warm up before you remove it.

You want your images to say "cold," so look for details that communicate that feeling. Ice-coated branches or berries, wind whipped snow over a mountain pass—any detail you can include in the photograph will help convey the message.

Storms

Photographers love storms. The dramatic skies, high winds, and horizontal rain make for very dramatic images. You can often get a good image of an otherwise dull landscape if there is a great stormy sky over it; the sky becomes the subject. Feel the power of a storm when you are in it, and find ways to convey that intensity with your camera.

Using a tripod and a
slow shutter speed, the
photographer was able
to render the waves
moving up this Big Sur
beach as ghostly.

Look around for subjects that really show the power of the storm, and then find ways to compose that accentuate the effects the weather is having on those subjects. The main thing to think about is exposure, for various expo-

sures can make the same storm scene look quite different. Do you want to freeze tree branches bent by the wind, or let them blur?

Consider what you want the image to look like, then determine the exposure that will achieve the effect: If you want horizontal rain slashing through the frame, use a slow enough shutter speed to let it streak a bit. A tornado calls for a fast speed to catch the action.

The sky is usually an important element of storm pictures, but be careful metering. A very dark sky can fool the camera meter into overexposing the whole scene. If you are photographing shafts of sunlight piercing the clouds, don't take your reading from them, or the meter will underexpose. Always look for something of neutral tonal value to meter, or use a gray card.

Lightning

If there is lightning in the scene, you'll have to be patient as well as lucky: You never know where lightning is going to strike. Make sure it doesn't strike you. Don't stand under trees, avoid metal fences and pipes, and be sure to stay low to the ground.

TIP:
Don't leave a long lens pointed directly into the sun for too long—you run the risk of burning a hole in the shutter just the way a magnifying glass can set a piece of paper on fire.

If you are taking photographs of lightning at night, put your camera on a tripod, set the shutter speed to bulb, choose a lens that encompasses a large enough area to give yourself a reasonable chance, and use an f-stop of 5.6 for low ISO or 8 or 11 for high ISO.

Aim your camera at the part of the sky where the lightning is, focus on infinity, and keep the shutter open for several lightning flashes. If it is early enough in the evening so that there is still some light in the sky, or if you are near an urban area, you will need to limit your exposure to between 5 and 20 seconds because of the ambient light.

If you are photographing a landscape with lightning during the daytime, you can't leave the shutter open as long as at night. To give yourself the best chance of capturing daytime flashes, figure out what the exposure time is for your smallest aperture (usually f/22), mount the camera on a tripod, and hope that you get lucky. For both daytime and nighttime photographs, make several exposures.

SUNSET AND SUNRISE

When shooting sunrises and sunsets, be very careful with metering, because the meter will want to underexpose. The ball of the sun will be very bright on clear days, and at sunrise you will have only a few seconds to shoot before the sun becomes too bright to photograph.

Cloudy or hazy days are actually the best for shooting, as cloud and haze diffuse the light, add more colors to the sky, and make the solar disk softer and more photographable for a longer time. But even when the sun is

softened by clouds or haze, don't meter directly at it. Look for mid-tones. In most cases, metering in the area of sky about 45 degrees away from the sun should be about right. It's always best to bracket sunrise and sunset shots to ensure getting the right exposure.

If you are photographing with a wide-angle lens, the rising or setting sun will be a rather small element of the image. The effect may be just what you want if the rest of the scene is beautifully lit and the sky is full of colors. If you would like the sun to be big, use a telephoto, and look for something to silhouette against it or a part of the sky near it. The longer the lens, the larger the sun will appear in the frame.

If you want detail rather than a silhouette of a subject in the foreground, you will have to use a reflector or fill-in flash to illuminate it. If using a flash, set it to under-expose somewhat (say 1/3 or 2/3 of a stop) to soften the contrast a bit. You usually don't want to overpower the feeling of the early or late light.

As with any photograph, think about composition and how your image can say something about the location. A telephoto shot of a rising or setting sun on its own is not all that interesting—it could be taken anywhere. Look for elements in the scene or in the sky that will communicate the sense of place.

Just Before and After Sunset and Sunrise

You will usually have a little bit of time to shoot landscapes in the soft, diffuse light before sunrise and after sunset. How much time depends upon the weather, the season, and the part of the world you are in.

It's a good idea to scout locations for this kind of shot beforehand to find appropriate scenes. Dark green forests usually don't register very well, while sand or snow scenes will. These will require exposures that are quite long, so use a tripod.

Be careful metering. Find the neutral tone or use a gray card. You are usually looking for that moment when the light in the sky and the light on the ground are balanced, and it doesn't last long.

Look for something—a stand of trees on a ridge, an interesting rock formation, or a city roofline to silhouette against the royal blue of a cloudless sky before sunrise on a clear day or against the pinks and oranges lighting up the sky on a cloudy one. The part of the sky where the sun is about to rise (or has just set) will be brighter than the rest of the sky, so meter about 45 degrees away from it.

Think about making photographs with silhouettes, too. Wait to shoot them until your subject stands out in contrast to the sky. Sometimes, especially if the landscape includes water, you may have a combination of bright and dark spots in the scene. Meter on something of neutral tone and cast your silhouette against one of

the brighter areas. Be sure to bracket. These are tricky shots, especially with transparency film.

NIGHT

You can't shoot landscapes or anything else without at least some light, so night shots are best made when there is a full or almost full moon. These shots work best when the scene has at least some fairly bright, reflective areas, especially when these throw light up behind darker ones. They require very long exposures: about 4 minutes for ISO 50–100, 2 minutes for ISO 125–200, and about 30 seconds for ISO 250–400. If the scene includes snow or white sand, cut the exposures in half and bracket.

If you are including the moon in your shot, do not expose for longer than 1/4 second or the moon will streak into an oblong white mass. The distortion becomes more noticeable the longer the lens. The best time to make landscapes that include the moon is when it rises near sunset. There will be plenty of ambient light on the land, and the moon will be low and appear large. Try to compose using something other than a wide-angle lens if you want the moon to be more than a white dot.

If you're photographing the moon itself, use a long

Mark Thiessen employed a few friends with flashlights to help him illuminate the darkening landscape around the Palomar Observatory in California.

lens or a telescope, many of which have camera mounts. You can also silhouette subjects against the moon. Be sure that you expose properly; the in-camera meter will tend to underexpose the bright surface of the moon. Open up and bracket.

Photographing star trails across the sky requires exposures of 15 minutes to several hours, depending upon how much of the arcs you want. Use a high ISO,

Park City, Utah, glows like gems in the snowy mountains. A glow in the sky was strong enough to barely light the snow, and the photographer made the image with a slow shutter speed to bring out the lights.

open the diaphragm all the way, and focus on infinity. Star trails are best photographed on clear, moonless nights away from the light pollution of urban areas. If you would like to include circular star trails in your image, point your camera at the North Star. Try silhouetting a tree or some other subject against a starry sky. This requires some experimentation, but the results can be beautiful.

PHOTOGRAPHY AS A STATE OF MIND

When he was 13 years old, Bruce Dale concocted a close-up camera out of an old roll-film Kodak, eyeglass lenses, and tissue paper so he could make an image of a flower. By graduation from high school he had already published more than 50 photographs in the *Toledo Blade*, an Ohio newspaper that later hired him. In 1964 he began a 30-year career at *National Geographic* magazine.

One of the hallmarks of Dale's long career at *Geographic* was his evocative work with landscapes all over the world. "When I have an assignment to photograph a new place," he says, "I do a lot of research. I look at postcards, books, Web sites, anything I can find on the place. If there is art or literature—poems, stories, diaries of people who lived there—I study that, too. I want to learn not just what a place looks like, but what it feels like and how it has struck other people.

"I set out with certain goals in mind, but those are not what I'm really looking for," says Dale. "Some of my favorite pictures I made on my way to the places everyone goes. I've always had good luck following my instincts, but photography really is a state of mind. If you're not in the right frame of mind, pictures can pop up all around you but you can't see them. You have to have a feeling for the place, to be open to it."

Traveling through the Southwest, Dale prefers to meander along back roads. "By just taking my time and keeping my eyes open, I discover something new every day."

Dale has now switched almost exclusively to digital cameras, but the elements of photography have not changed. "A good landscape image, like any photograph, is largely about relationships and perspective," he says. "Most people think that when they are shooting a wide scene they should use a wide lens, but that is often not the case. It's natural to try to include everything, but you have to think about how objects relate to each other within the frame. Do you really want to include *everything* in the photo? Be selective, then try backing up and using a 50mm or 85mm lens to get a more pleasing perspective. I've made a lot of successful images this way, even though they look as if they were made with a 28mm lens."

"You have to learn to see as your camera does," continues

A frame within a frame and strong graphic elements reinforce the rugged beauty of this western landscape.

Dale. "If you squint, or look at a scene through a heavy neutral density filter, you can cut down on the visual range your eye sees and more closely simulate the way your camera will capture the scene. I also find it very helpful to close one eye. It eliminates the stereoscopic effect and puts you on the same two-dimensional plane as the photograph. Notice how the scene changes when you move even an inch or two.

"What's really important is to be open to the feeling of a place, to slow down and allow it in. Look at the scene from several angles, have the patience to wait for the right light, and if necessary return several times to find that magical moment."

Vanishing point: A bridge and its perfect reflection fade into the fog of a Missouri lake.

Composition in blue and white: A church in New Mexico points toward a wispy sky.

Chapter 4
Cameras & Lenses

4 | *Cameras & Lenses*

Digital SLR cameras have the same look, feel, and accessories as their 35mm film predecessors.

Previous pages:
A long time exposure at night encircles a mountain in Chad with stars.

Photography is in the midst of a remarkable revolution. The advent of digital cameras and imaging, editing, and archiving software has profoundly changed the ease and speed with which we can make and view our pictures, what we can do with them, and how we keep them.

The actual making of photographs hasn't really changed. Light passes through a lens, and a diaphragm controls the amount; a variable-speed shutter determines the length of time the light gets through. From that point, one important thing does change. In digital cameras, the light hits a sensor rather than film. Everything else about making good photographs—especially the most important part, looking and thinking—is exactly the same. Remember: Cameras, no matter what type or how advanced, don't make pictures. You do.

CHOOSING THE FORMAT

Whether you shoot on film or digital cards, you have a choice of camera types. Large- and medium-format cameras have long been the preference of serious landscape photographers. The advantage of larger-format cameras is simple—the larger the film or sensor, the greater the capacity to record detail. Both formats now offer models that are fully digital or that can be equipped with digital backs. Panoramic cameras are available in both film and digital models.

Large-format, medium-format, and panoramic cameras are specialized and expensive pieces of equipment. Developing the skill needed to properly use a large-format view camera requires patience and dedication. The results can be stunning, but such specialized equipment is really only for the most serious enthusiasts. Most of us want to get good landscape photographs with the gear we already have or plan to buy for general purposes. So I will focus on the most common types of cameras—compacts and SLRs (*single-lens reflex* refers to the fact that the photographer and the sensor see the subject through the same lens).

FILM CAMERAS

Until recently, the 35mm SLR camera was the most popular choice of both serious amateur and professional photographers. SLR cameras and accessories are small enough to be easily portable, and a wide range of

Photographer Gordon Wiltsie is as skilled as his subject to make this image in Canada.

lenses, strobes, and other add-ons are available in a range of prices from inexpensive to very dear. The 35mm film format (actually 24 X 36mm) is large enough to make excellent large prints and offers the widest range of film types.

In recent years, digital SLRs have become more prevalent than film SLRs, so I'll go into more detail about the advantages of digital SLRs in the section below. But if you want to shoot on film and you're going to have one camera system for landscapes, portraits, and other photographs, the 35mm SLR is a good choice.

The 35mm rangefinder camera offers superb optics, small size, and quiet operation—attributes that make these cameras popular with photojournalists and travel photographers who want to make images of people in an unobtrusive way. For landscape photography, though, they are not ideal. The fact that you do not see through the same lens that the film does makes extreme close-up framing difficult. You cannot check depth of field or see the effects of polarizing filters, and there are no long telephoto or close-focusing lenses available.

Compact (point-and-shoot) film cameras are not really suited to serious landscape photography, and they have been waning in popularity anyway. In the United States they are increasingly being replaced with digital compacts.

DIGITAL CAMERAS

Digital SLR cameras look and feel almost exactly like the 35mm film SLRs on which they were modeled. They offer a wide array of interchangeable lenses, external flash units, and many other accessories. Most have several automated settings with sophisticated multisample metering and highly accurate autofocus. They can make properly exposed and sharply focused pictures in a variety of ways, but they also allow overrides of the automated features so that you can have increasing control in making images as your skill and experience grow. In full manual mode you can have complete control of the process.

With a single-lens reflex camera, what you see in the viewfinder is what you get. This is particularly useful in careful compositions where there is a risk of unwanted elements sneaking into the edges of the frame and also in close-up work. You can see the effects of polarizing or other filters and, in most models, preview depth of field.

Digital SLRs have many advantages over film SLRs. The most obvious one is that you can see the image as soon as you've made it rather than wait for film to come back from the lab. This is a great aid in tricky lighting situations and for experimenting. Most photographic printing these days is done from electronic files, and film shooters will usually find that they have to scan their images before printing. Digital cameras make this rather expensive step unnecessary.

Another nice feature of digital photography is that you can shoot in any situation. When using film, it might be necessary to change from a slow film to a fast one when moving indoors or shooting at dusk. Photographing an interior might mean changing from outdoor light-balanced film to tungsten. Digital cameras make these situations easy to handle. Simply change the ISO rating from one frame to the next, or change the white balance as required.

With film cameras, one of the main determinants of image quality is the size of the film and the amount of grain (slow films have less grain than fast ones). In the digital world, quality is determined largely by the number

TIP:
A good camera bag is important for working in the field. You want one that is comfortable to carry and the right size for all your gear.

Opposite page:
Four images show the relative sizes of some common film formats, from 35mm to 6 X 17cm. The larger the film or sensor, the finer the detail, which is important if you're making larger prints. Larger formats, however, require more cumbersome gear.

TIP:
Many cameras have built-in diopter adjustment. If yours does not, you can usually buy an eyesight-compensation lens that attaches to the camera eyepiece.

of pixels a camera's sensor can hold and is expressed as a given model's megapixel (a million pixels) rating. More pixels usually means finer detail, and this holds true for both compact cameras and SLRs.

COMPACT DIGITAL CAMERAS

Compact digital cameras are radically different from their film ancestors, which were limited to snapshot use. They come in a huge range of prices and features, from the simplest point-and-shoot to the very sophisticated. Those at the bottom end are usually in the lower megapixel range and have limited zoom capabilities and only automated shooting modes, which limit creativity. The higher-end cameras have shutter and aperture priority modes and the option of fully manual controls. The sensors have greater capacity and the zoom lenses have greater reach. You can manually adjust ISO rating and white balance. The lack of interchangeable lenses and external flash units are the only real limits on your creativity.

The image quality of the higher-end digital compact cameras is excellent. If you don't want to lug around a camera bag full of gear but want something that fits in your shirt pocket instead, a compact is a good choice.

KEY TERMS IN
DIGITAL PHOTOGRAPHY
Megapixel

Digital cameras are largely defined by their megapixel ratings. A 12-megapixel camera will record more information than a 3-megapixel camera. There's a tendency to think that more is better, but there's a limit to how many pixels you actually need. A 3-megapixel camera will yield just as good an 8 X 10 print as its big brother. You only need a certain amount of information for any given print size. It's important to consider what you ultimately want to do with your pictures. The higher the megapixel rating, the more expensive the camera, and there's no need to buy more camera than you

Compact digital cameras have many features and great optics.

think you'll really use.

If you shoot for the Web, e-mail, or 4 X 6 prints, a 3-megapixel camera is more than enough. If you want to

DIGITAL VERSUS OPTICAL ZOOM

Digital zoom renders the upper close-up of this sign fuzzy.

A word of caution about compact cameras: Most of these are equipped with lenses that offer two zoom modes—optical and digital. You should limit yourself to using only the optical zoom. When the optics inside a lens zoom in, they magnify the subject so that it takes up a larger percentage of the frame and therefore of the sensor. Digital zoom does not increase the size of the subject, but simply crops away the area around it and then, through algorithmic interpolations, blows up the middle to fill the frame. In the process, the amount of detail in the subject is greatly reduced, and in large prints especially, the image will look fuzzy.

If you think your subject is too small, the best solution is to get closer. Wade in water, climb a cliff, do whatever it takes within reason. If you can't move in close enough to your subject, use the maximum extension of your optical zoom lens. Use digital zoom only when you really can't do anything else.

make large prints or crop in a lot, you will need more megapixels.

But megapixels alone are not the whole story. The quality of the sensor and the internal processing are just as important. Larger-megapixel cameras usually have higher-quality circuits and more sophisticated algorithms that produce better color and less "noise," which is seen as grain in the images. In compact cameras, more can actually be worse: Cramming more pixels onto the same-sized sensor can result in greater noise, and you may actually get a better image from a 3-

megapixel camera than from a 5. Before purchasing a camera, talk to your local dealer and check out reviews and opinions on the Web.

ISO

The ISO (International Organization for Standardization) originally rated the light sensitivity of film. Now ISO ratings are used to indicate the sensitivity of a sensor for digital photography. High ISO numbers mean high sensitivity, which is useful when taking pictures in low-light situations.

A wide-angle lens allows great depth of field to render the leading lines of plowed and unplowed earth as well as the tractor at work.

File Formats

The most commonly used file format for digital image storage is JPEG (Joint Photographic Experts Group), which uses algorithms to compress digital information and reduce the size of picture files. JPEG compression requires that some information be thrown out, and how much depends on which JPEG setting you choose—small, medium, or large. Be aware that every time you open and close JPEGs more information is lost, unless they are stored on a permanent medium such as CDs or DVDs.

Many cameras also offer the option of storing images in TIFF (Tagged Image File Format) files, and high-end cameras offer RAW (unprocessed) files. Both of these are of higher quality than JPEGs but take up much more room on memory cards.

White Balance

This adjustment to the way an image is processed compensates for different light sources so that white is reproduced as white.

WIDE-ANGLE LENSES

Landscape photographs are most often made with wide-angle lenses for the simple reason that you can see more of the scene through them. They also have the advantage of great depth of field, so it's not difficult to have all the layers of a scene in sharp focus. There are several things you should keep in mind, though, when using any lens with a focal length shorter than 50mm—and the shorter the focal length, the more pronounced the effects will be. (We use 50mm lenses as the "standard" in the 35mm format because they record subjects about the same size as we see them.) The best advice when selecting a lens for a particular scene is, as always, look carefully and think. Is what you see through the viewfinder what you really want? If not, use a different lens or find a location that works better.

Include a Point of Interest

As we discussed earlier, the most common failing of landscape photographs is the lack of a clear point of interest. Because a wide-angle lens takes in such a wide area, and because every element within it is usually in focus, the images can be flat and boring unless you are careful to compose them in a dynamic way. Often,

TRAVELING WITH DIGITAL GEAR

Though going digital has lots of advantages, it means carrying more when traveling. In the old days, I could go out on assignment with a camera, a few lenses, and some rolls of film. At night, after I finished shooting, I could enjoy a leisurely dinner. Now nights are occupied by downloading, backing up, entering keywords, and recharging. Those processes mean more stuff to lug along.

For me, the following are essentials to pack:

- A laptop computer allows you to download images to free up memory cards for reuse. It will also enable you to view your images on something larger than your camera's LCD. To be safe, you can use your laptop to burn backup CDs or DVDs of your photos. A portable hard drive will offer additional backup.
- Extra memory cards are a must because it's impossible to predict exactly how much memory you'll need.
- Include a cable that connects your camera to your laptop or portable hard drive. Or take a card reader that connects to your laptop, usually through a USB port.
- Bring extra batteries. Most electronic gear relies on rechargeable batteries, and there are few things worse than running out of juice at a critical moment. Take extras for your camera, laptop, and portable hard drive, and be sure to recharge every night. If you'll be away from a power outlet, take an adapter that works off your car's cigarette lighter. If you'll even be a distance from cars, take a solar charger or lots and lots of batteries.

A wide-angle shot of a temple in Nepal is fairly nondescript (top). A 300mm lens made the temple stand out and drew the cliffs closer so that they appear to loom above it (bottom).

everything is there but nothing stands out.

Foreground elements, leading lines, and other compositional techniques we have discussed help overcome this tendency of wide-angle lenses to include too much. Think about what is most important in the frame, then use compositional techniques and the positive qualities of wide-angles to guide your viewers to it. You want to include enough of the setting to get a feel for the place, but not so much that you lose the point.

Perspective and Distortion

Distance to a subject controls perspective, not the focal length of a lens. But wide-angle lenses tend to exaggerate perspective because they allow us to get a close subject and a distant one in focus at the same time. They exaggerate relationships by expanding the apparent distance between nearby and distant objects. Wide-angle lenses seem to enlarge near subjects and diminish those that are far away, and the shorter the lens, the greater this effect. These lenses also tend to elongate subjects that are near the edges of the frame. You can use these qualities to create very dynamic images—of a huge moss-covered boulder in a valley with a mountain peak rising behind it, for instance. Avoid using a lens that is too short, though. You don't want to push the mountaintop so far back that it becomes insignificant.

If wide-angles are tilted up or down even slightly, they will distort any vertical lines within the frame, making them appear as if they are converging. It's an effect known as "keystoning" and is particularly noticeable with buildings. When photographing natural subjects, keystoning is not usually much of a problem, since there are not many straight lines in nature.

The tendency of wide-angle lenses to distort is only a problem if it creates an effect that you do not want. Become familiar with the way different lenses work, and then employ them to get the photographs you want.

Depth of Field with Wide-Angle Lenses

Wide-angle lenses have great depth of field, and again, the shorter the focal length, the greater the range. You should have no problem keeping all the elements of your image in sharp focus, unless you are including something that is very close to the lens. If you are doing this, check the depth of field—with the preview button if your camera has one—to make sure you are getting what you want. If your camera lacks a preview button, use a smaller aperture and slower shutter speed (the smaller the aperture, the greater the depth of field). If this necessitates a shutter speed slower than 1/60, you will have to use a tripod or other camera-steadying device.

Be conscious of wind. If a flower or tree is an important foreground element, even a slight wind will blur it at slow shutter speeds. An advantage to shooting early in the morning, besides the great light, is that there is usually no wind. Conversely, if you want one element to really stand out, you may not want all the elements within the frame to be in sharp focus. If too much of a scene is in sharp focus, open up the aperture and use a faster shutter speed.

TELEPHOTO LENSES

Telephoto lenses have the opposite effect of wide-angles: They make objects appear closer and larger and compress the apparent distances between them. Telephotos have a narrower angle of view than a normal or a wide-angle lens, so they take in a smaller area of a scene.

The longer the focal length, the greater the effect. Telephotos range from 85mm up to 600mm or even longer, and the field of view gets narrower as focal length increases. In many cases, telephotos can enhance the compositional techniques we discussed earlier: They can make your subject fill a foreground frame, accentuate leading lines and patterns, and make it easier to exclude unwanted elements. They are also useful if you simply cannot get physically closer to your subject.

Scanning

Whenever you're shooting, even if you plan to make only a wide-angle image, get out a telephoto and scan around. You will often discover things you had not seen with your naked eye or with a wide-angle lens. If you have a telephoto zoom, look at the scene through varying focal lengths to see how they affect it. Look for details and to see how the lens compresses elements

within the frame. Use the properties of telephoto lenses to isolate interesting elements or to create graphic images using lines or contrast.

Perspective and Compression

Telephoto lenses seem to compress, or "stack," objects within the frame, making them appear to be larger and closer together than they really are. We've all seen images of a range of mountaintops or row of tree trunks made with telephotos in which the objects seem to be jammed together. This is a useful and often dramatic technique. But there is another type of compression that you should think about.

In the example we've used in other chapters, the farmhouse on the prairie, let's suppose there's a mountain in the background. If you photograph the scene with a wide-angle lens, the mountain will seem far away from the farmhouse and rather small. This will yield the feeling of isolation that you're after. But if you back off and use a long lens, the two will be compressed together so that the mountain appears to loom over the farmhouse. This image will give you a very different feeling.

TIP:
Shoot a row of tree trunks with a wide-angle lens and a telephoto lens and compare the results to see how compression works.

Depth of Field with Telephoto Lenses

Telephotos have very little depth of field, and the longer the lens, the less there is. Be very careful focusing, and be sure that the point of interest in the frame is sharp. Decide beforehand what you want to be in focus and what you don't, then check the depth of field to be sure the image will be what you want.

You may or may not want the whole frame to be sharp. A good exercise is to shoot a row of tree trunks. If they are all pretty much the same, you might want them all to be in focus so that the image becomes one of vertical lines and the patterns on the bark. To get all the tree trunks in focus, use a small aperture, slow shutter speed, and probably a tripod.

If one of the trees has a new leaf emerging, or some other interesting detail, you might want only it to be sharp and the others to be out of focus. In such a case, be sure to compose carefully. Remember the rule of thirds and use a large aperture and fast shutter speed.

Isolating Detail

Always be on the lookout for nature's gorgeous details. Often one interesting detail can say as much or more about a place as a wide view can. Icicles on a branch might say "winter" better than a shot of the whole tree. Telephoto lenses are particularly good for isolating details, especially of things you can't get near. View the entire scene through a telephoto, then boil the experience down to one detail.

The woman and child in the top image give both scale and an active sense of looking to this coastal scene. Without them, the photograph is less interesting.

When shooting details with long lenses, watch exposure, focus, and movement. Think about the tonal quality of whatever fills your frame. If it looks lighter or darker than neutral gray, you'll have to compensate exposure. Telephotos have very little depth of field when close-focused, so be sure to get the right aperture/shutter speed combination for the effect you want.

Long lenses exaggerate even tiny movement. You'll probably need a tripod if shooting slow shutter speeds. With telephotos a slow shutter speed means anything slower than 1/250 or 1/500 because their weight and length make them difficult to hold steady. If you don't have a remote release, use the timer so you can make the image without your finger jiggling the camera.

Chapter 5
Digital Strategies

5 *Digital Strategies*

Strong bands of color in the sky, in the trees, and on the ground add drama to this photograph of autumn foliage.

Previous pages: The sweeping sand beneath the green water of a bay at Cape Cod makes an abstract background for a small sailboat.

Opposite page: A slow shutter speed records the dim light in the tent and the glow of the moon over campers in Pakistan.

WORKING IN A NEW WAY

Digital photography has opened up a new world in terms of what we can do to and with our photographs. No more darkrooms and noxious chemicals—all you need now is a computer and the software that comes rich with editing features. Here are some simple but important things you should become familiar with.

MANAGING COLOR

Color is one of the trickiest aspects of photography because it's subject to so many variables. Different films render the same color differently, as do different sensors and their processors. Lens quality can have dramatic effect on how wavelengths of light (colors) are transmitted.

The color temperature of light falling on the subject when the picture was made also matters a great deal. A scene shot in full sunlight looks different from the same subject on a cloudy day, and thick clouds make it look different from thin ones. This is due to the wavelength of the light, with longer waves being more red, shorter ones more blue. Because we perceive warm light as being "prettier," we tend to like pictures made in the warmer light of early morning and late afternoon to those made in the cooler light of midday. You can greatly affect how your pictures look and feel simply by thinking about what light or what time of day you want to make them in.

In the end, as the photographer, you're the only one who knows what a scene should look like because you saw it in real life. The point is to get your finished image to look as much like the real scene as possible.

AT THE COMPUTER

When you're working digitally, you want the print that emerges from your printer to look like what you see on your screen. It's important to calibrate your monitor. Many computers come with calibration software, but if you plan to print a lot of photos, it's worth investing in a calibrator that reads the colors on your monitor and creates a color profile for it. If your monitor is not calibrated, you can end up with

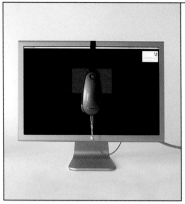

Monitor calibration is essential for getting good prints and for sharing images.

some very odd-looking prints. (Trust me, I've produced plenty of them.) As you work with your image, recall what the scene looked like and try to duplicate it, keeping in mind that color is a pretty subjective thing. Your photograph should be one you like and are happy with.

There are entire books about color management that give detailed information. I'll mention some fairly simple operations that will make your images look better. Experiment—in digital photography, anything you do can be undone; the best way to learn is by trying.

Before you do anything else, back up your images, preferably on a CD, DVD, or other such medium. There's always a chance that you'll press "return" before you mean to, saving unwanted changes, and hard drives inevitably crash. If you have a backup (two are even better, one kept in another location), you won't jump out the window when you hear a grinding noise or see smoke coming from your computer.

In the example here, I used Adobe Photoshop®, a popular choice among photographers. Many imaging programs are included with digital cameras. Some computers come with them, and there are many stand-alones available. All have features for enhancing your pictures, though they may go by different names.

After you've calibrated your monitor and opened your image, the first thing to try is Auto Levels, under the Image > Adjustments menu in Photoshop. (In other programs it might be called Enhance or something similar.) The software will read the image and automatically make adjustments. Sometimes this is all it takes to bring out the colors, contrast, and brightness of an image.

If Auto Levels doesn't work, try the other automated adjustments. If you're still not happy, most programs offer tools for adjusting brightness, contrast, color saturation, and tint. Play with these until you're happy with the way the image looks. When you're finished, save as a different file so you can go back to the original if you need to.

Using Histograms

Histograms have become the light meters of the digital world. They offer a way to see whether you have gotten the right exposure for your image. In most cases you can see right away, as they can be viewed in your camera's LCD screen. Histograms might look complicated, but they really aren't. You need to be able to read them if you want to make good photographs.

A histogram is a graphic representation of the exposure in an image. The amount of information in different tonal ranges is shown by the height of the bars, from black on the left to white on the right. Most images will show the highest bars and most information in the middle, the midtone range.

In an image that has the entire gamut of colors from black to white, the histogram will begin at the bottom left corner and end at the bottom right corner. This shows that the blackest blacks and whitest whites are captured in the image. If the bars on either the left or right are not at the bottom of the graph, it means that detail in the darkest or lightest areas is lost—there is no true black or white. A flat line indicates a lack of data in that area. The example on page 144 shows histograms of the same subject that are overexposed, underexposed, and properly exposed.

After you've downloaded your images into your computer and opened them with your software, have a look at the histogram. If you're not happy with the way the image looks, here are two quick ways to improve it.

1. Drag the triangle at bottom left toward the middle of the histogram until it's below the first bar on the left, then do the same for the triangle representing white on the right. This will make the darkest part of your image black and the lightest part white.

2. If your software includes eyedroppers for sampling the image, use the black one to sample the darkest area and the white one to sample the lightest. Like dragging the triangles, this will set black and white points for the image.

Adjustments can bring out details.

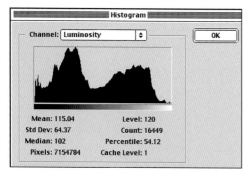

Channel: Luminosity	OK

Mean: 115.04	Level: 120
Std Dev: 64.37	Count: 16449
Median: 102	Percentile: 54.12
Pixels: 7154784	Cache Level: 1

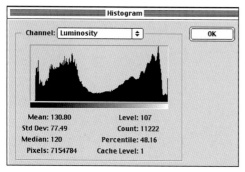

Channel: Luminosity	OK

Mean: 130.80	Level: 107
Std Dev: 77.49	Count: 11222
Median: 120	Percentile: 48.16
Pixels: 7154784	Cache Level: 1

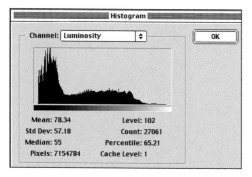

Channel: Luminosity	OK

Mean: 78.34	Level: 102
Std Dev: 57.18	Count: 27061
Median: 55	Percentile: 65.21
Pixels: 7154784	Cache Level: 1

Histograms graphically show overexposure (top), proper exposure (middle) and underexposure (bottom) in these shots of flowers. You can check histograms on the viewers of many cameras.

SORTING AS YOU GO

Most of us have shoeboxes, drawers, perhaps even closets stuffed with slides and envelopes of prints and negatives. We might pull a few pictures to put in albums or stick on the refrigerator, but most of our pictures end up stashed away for that rainy day when we will organize them. The number of those paper and celluloid pictures may seem overwhelming, but it pales in comparison to the images we're amassing in the digital age. In 2003, consumers had an average of 750 photographs on their computers. That number has grown to over 7,000 and keeps rising. Film costs money every time we press the shutter button, but once we've purchased a memory card for our digital camera, it costs nothing to take more pictures, so we do. The bottleneck happens when we're not sure what to do with them. How to sort through and edit images is a major challenge today.

There are many things you can do with the images on your memory card. If you're taking snapshots of the family vacation, you can simply take the card to a local photo shop or drugstore and plug it into one of the photo kiosks that have recently become ubiquitous. These accept all sorts of memory cards, as well as CDs and DVDs, and will automatically produce all or a selection of pictures on wallet-size, 4 x 6, 5 x 7, or 8 x 10 paper.

Don't forget to label your CDs and DVDs (above). Photo kiosks at drugstores and other locations accept all sorts of media.

Several companies make personal photo printers that work much the same way; simply plug in your camera via a USB cord or insert your card, select the pictures and settings you want (with or without a border, etc.), and print. These printers do a remarkably good job.

TIP:

If you have more images than will reasonably fit on a 5 X 5 jewel case contact sheet, make two—one facing out and the other inside the lid.

Many image-editing programs (Apple's Aperture™ in this case) allow you to view selections and choices at the same time, making editing an easier task.

Most are limited to 4 X 6 paper, though some do 5 X 7s as well. If you want to make larger prints, refine your images, or share them through e-mail or a Web site, you'll need to download them into your computer.

BACKING UP—A CRUCIAL STEP

First, back up your images on a second hard drive, CD, DVD, or other medium. The hard drive in your computer will crash someday. This is not just a probability said simply to scare you, but a certainty. If you don't have a backup, all your images will be lost. Most photographers keep at least two backups—one in their studio and one at another location. You can never have too many.

Backing up is easy; most CD- and DVD-burning programs work as a simple drag and drop. Once you have dragged folders from your memory card to the copy medium, rename them with the location, event, or date. The folders on your memory card will read 100NCD2X, 120 CANON, 100HP817, or something equally unhelpful. Giving them names that mean something to you and a date will make them much easier to identify.

To make finding the right backup CD or DVD easy, make contact sheets. Many software programs offer a way

MY OWN SYSTEM FOR SAVING PHOTOS

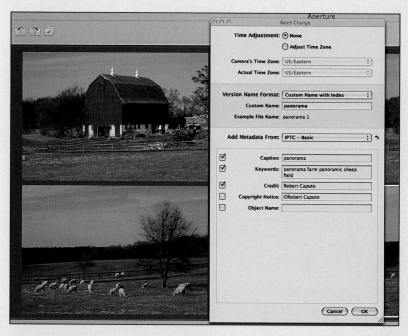

Using batch functions makes the editing task more efficient.

After backing up images on CDs or DVDs, I import them into a photo-editing program—Aperture is shown here, but most software works in similar ways. By creating a new folder for the pictures, "landscapes bk_panoramas," I have already made them easy to find as a group. They are also automatically entered into Aperture's library along with all the other photographs I've imported.

The next step is to give the images names more meaningful than DSC_001.NEF (NEF is Nikon's RAW format). I do this with "Batch Change," which also allows me to attach keywords, copyright notice, and other information. By selecting all the images in the folder before the batch change, I can do them all at once.

After viewing the images at a reasonable size and deciding which ones I want to use for a panorama, I select them and give them a five-star rating. The stars show up on the frames, making them easy to identify quickly. Double-clicking on one of the five selected images opens them in Photoshop (most editing programs offer you a choice of opening images in their own editor or in a different one you've selected).

Once in Photoshop, I can create panoramas like the one on pages 66–67.

to do this and give options for the size of the contact sheet, the thumbnails, and the numbers of rows and columns. Print on regular letter-size paper and keep these in a binder with the CD or DVD number on them. Better yet, make them 5 x 5 and slip them inside the covers of the jewel cases.

METADATA AND MORE

Most new computers and digital cameras are packaged with photo-viewing applications, some of which also do image editing such as cropping, red-eye reduction, color enhancement, and so on. There are also several stand-alone applications. All of these take advantage of our computers' capacity to search and the ease with which names and other information (called metadata) can be attached to our

pictures. Digital cameras automatically attach certain metadata to each image: date, time, camera, exposure, flash on or off—the list goes on. Much of this is useful. If you are looking for a photograph you made on a trip to the Grand Canyon in July 2005, enter the date into your software's search engine to narrow the search down to a reasonable number of images.

If you really want to get control of your pictures, it's worth spending some time adding to the metadata attached by your camera. Many image-browsing programs have easy ways to enter keywords. Some offer lists of common subjects like "family," "kids," "vacation," or "birthday" that you simply click on. Some allow you to make up your own keywords, and most offer a star or other kind of rating option.

BATCH EDITING

You can batch-edit your pictures, entering the same keywords for many frames so you don't have to do them one by one. The best time to enter keywords is as soon as possible, on your trip if you have a laptop along, or as soon as you get home. You're likely to remember more details earlier on, and you're less likely to do it at all later as the trips and photos pile up.

You should also batch-edit the names of your images. Like the names of the folders on your memory card, the camera-assigned names are meaningless—IMG_1779.JPG or DSC_0096.JPG, and so on. Using a batch renaming function, you can easily change these to Yellowstone_001.JPG, etc. Many programs give you choices for names, numbers, and extensions. Another advantage of renaming all the images is avoiding the possibility of repetition. Every time you format your memory card, your camera will begin numbering pictures from the same point, and you will end up with dozens of DSC_012s.

When clouds have interesting shapes and colors, include them in aerials, even though aerials are more often shot looking down.

Backing up and entering keywords may seem like a lot of work, and in fact it is. But it will pay off later by saving you a lot of time. The frustration of rummaging manually through thousands of digital files is not unlike digging through a drawer full of prints. Once you've entered key-

words for your images, you will have powerful tools that will help you find them easily.

RATING IMAGES

Now that you have backed up and renamed your folders and images and entered keywords, there is still a bit of work to do. A search for a specific subject or date will turn up a few—or a few dozen—pictures. You still need to sort through them to find the best.

Most image-browsing programs have a feature that emulates the light tables that were used for decades to sort and edit slides. You can double-click on an image to increase its size and view it in some detail. These programs also allow you to drag images around within the screen. Place like images next to one another so you can compare them. Once you have selected the best frame of a subject, tag it with a five-star rating. Do the same for other subjects, then tell the software to show you only five-star rated pictures, and voila, you will have a screen filled with your best shots. You can create a new album or folder that will include only these.

HOW THE SYSTEM WORKS

To get an idea of how the system works, say you shot 18 different scenes during a recent trip to Yellowstone, an average of 40 frames per scene. That makes 720 pictures—quite a lot to go through if they haven't been annotated, but fortunately you were thinking ahead. Each evening as you sat by the campfire you batch-entered keywords for the day's shoot.

Now at home, all of your pictures have been backed up, and you simply enter "Old Faithful" in the software's search engine. The 720 frames you shot are instantly winnowed down to just 65. You drag similar frames next to each other, select the best wide shot, close-up, etc., and give them each five stars. A few you are unsure of, so you give them four stars. You create new folders for the fours and fives and move on to the next batch of photos.

Once you've chosen your best frames, you can print them, e-mail them to friends, or put them up on a Web site. If you want to go back and make more prints, they will be easy to find. And when your hard drive crashes, you won't be worried because you've backed up everything and know exactly where to find your pictures.

Useful Information

EQUIPMENT
Camera Bag Essentials
camera bag lined with foam rubber compartments
camera body with body cap and neck strap
favorite lenses with lens caps
lens hoods
film of various ISO ratings or memory cards
  for digital cameras
air blower brush
lens cleaner solution and lens tissue wipes
tripod, monopod, and/or bean bags
gaffer's tape
electronic flash
batteries
remote release
equipment manuals

For Digital Photography Also Take:
laptop or external hard drive for backup
memory card reader
extra rechargeable batteries for camera and lap-
  top/external hard drive

Optional
filters, such as UV haze, skylight 1A, polarizing,
  neutral density, graded neutral density, light
  amber, light blue
plastic bag or sheet to protect equipment in wet
  weather
soft, absorbent towel or chamois
silica gel for wet weather
large umbrella
extra camera body
extra electronic flash
selenium cell exposure meter that operates in
  cold weather
notebook
sunglasses
head and wrist sweatbands
camouflage clothing for shooting landscapes
  with animals

resealable plastic bags for storing memory cards
  or film
18% gray card
customized diopter to match your eyeglass
  prescription
reflectors
slave units and radio transmitter for electronic
extension tubes
teleconverters

Tool Kit
Swiss Army knife
filter wrench
small socket wrenches
jeweler's screwdrivers
tweezers
needle-nosed pliers to loosen jammed tripod joints
pencil eraser to clean connections

Safety
flashlight
compass
whistle
water
snacks
first aid kit
reflective tape for clothing during nighttime
  shooting

ONLINE RESOURCES
The World Wide Web provides an almost limitless resource for landscape photographers, with sites for individual photographers, books, discussion groups, travel and weather information, scenic attractions, photographic equipment, how-to tips, and much more. Sometimes the information can be quite specific: If you are interested in shooting fall colors in New Hampshire, for example, the state Web site (www.newhampshire.com) will tell you when and where they are peaking. Use a search engine to find sites by photographer's name or keyword. The following is a list to get you started.

Keep in mind that site content can change or even vanish. There's no substitute for hunting around.

Websites
Raymond Gehman
www.blackdogphotographer.com
Joel Sartore
www.joelsartore.com
Bruce Dale
www.brucedale.com
American Society of Media Photographers
www.asmp.org
BestStuff.com
www.beststuff.com
Eastman Kodak Company
www.kodak.com
National Audubon Society
www.audubon.org
National Geographic Society
www.nationalgeographic.com
National Wildlife Federation
www.nwf.org
North American Nature Photography Association
www.nanpa.org
Robert Caputo
www.robertcaputo.com

Photo Books Online
Amazon
www.amazon.com
Barnes and Noble
www.barnesandnoble.com
Buy.com
www.buy.com

Photo Magazines Online
Apogee Online Photo magazine
www.apogeephoto.com
Camera Arts magazine
www.cameraarts.com
Nature's Best Photography magazine
www.naturesbestmagazine.com/
Outdoor Photographer magazine
www.outdoorphotographer.com
PC Photo magazine
www.pcphotomag.com

Photo District News magazine
www.pdnonline.com
Photo Life magazine (Canada)
www.photolife.com
Digital Photo Pro magazine
www.digitalphotopro.com
Popular Photography magazine
On AOL only; keyword: POP PHOTO
Shutterbug magazine
www.shutterbug.com

Photo Travel Guides and Tourism Online
Fodor's Focus on Travel Photography
www.fodors.com/focus
GORP: Great Outdoor Recreational Pages and Links (includes U.S. National Parks and Preserves by state)
www.gorp.com
Great Outdoor Recreational Pages, Canada (links to numerous federal and provincial sites)
www.gorp.com/gorp/location/canada/canada.htm
National Park Service
www.nps.gov
National Scenic Rivers
www.nps.gov/rivers
National Scenic Trails
www.nps.gov/trails
Parks Canada
www.pc.gc.ca
Photograph America Newsletter
www.photographamerica.com
PhotoSecret's Travel Guides for Travel Photography
www.photosecrets.com
Photo Traveler
www.phototravel.com
Professional Photographers of America (PPA)
www.ppa-world.org
State Tourism Information
www.statename.com
Tourism Canada
www.tourism-canada.com
Trail maps from National Geographic
www.trailsillustrated.com

Travel Canada
www.travel-library.com

USDA Forest Service National Headquarters
www.fs.fed.us

U.S. Department of State
www.state.gov

U.S. Fish and Wildlife Service Home Page
www.fws.gov

U.S. Photo Site Database/by State
www.viewcamera.com

Weather Channel
www.weather.com

Recreational Photography Forums

AOL Photography Forums
On AOL only; keyword: Photography on AOL:
rec.photo.technique.nature.com

CompuServe Photography Forums
On Compuserve "go photoforum"

Shaw Guides to Photo Tours and Workshops
www.shawguides.com

PHOTOGRAPHY MAGAZINES

Listed are photography magazines. Look at travel, scientific, and cultural ones, too, to see how other photographers have covered a place. Most magazines have websites.

American Photo. Monthly publication with features on professional photographers, photography innovations, and equipment reviews.

Camera Arts. Bimonthly magazine including portfolios, interviews, and equipment reviews.

Digital Camera. Bimonthly publication emphasizing digital cameras, imaging software, and accessories.

Digital Photographer. Quarterly publication emphasizing digital cameras, accessories, and technique.

Nature Photographer. Quarterly magazine about nature photography.

Nature's Best Photography. Quarterly magazine showcasing nature photography and profiling top professional photographers.

Outdoor & Nature Photography. Four issues a year. Heavily technique and equipment oriented with a strong "how to" approach.

Outdoor Photographer. Ten issues per year. Covers all aspects of photography outdoors, with articles about professional photographers, equipment, and techniques.

PC Photo. Bimonthly publication covering all facets of computers and photography.

Petersen's PHOTOgraphic. Monthly publication covering all facets of photography.

Photo District News. Monthly business magazine for professional photographers.

Photo Life. Bimonthly publication with limited availability in the U.S. Covers all facets of photography.

Photo Techniques. Monthly magazine dedicated to equipment.

PhotoWorld Magazine. Bimonthly publication dedicated to shooting, composition, lighting, processing, and printing.

Popular Photography. Monthly publication covering all facets of imaging, from conventional photography to digital. Heavily equipment oriented, with comprehensive test reports.

Shutterbug. Monthly publication covering all facets of photography from conventional to digital. Also includes numerous ads for used and collectible photo equipment.

View Camera. Bimonthly magazine covering all aspects of large-format photography.

PHOTOGRAPHY BOOKS

The following books are about photographic techniques, composition, and the like. Also look at books of landscape photographs and paintings, too numerous to list here but which you will find in any good bookstore or online.

General Photography Books

Cohen, Debbie, *Kodak Professional Photoguide*, Tiffen.

Doeffinger, Derek, *The Art of Seeing*, Kodak Workshop Series, Tiffen.

Eastman Kodak Co., *Kodak Guide to 35mm Photography*, Tiffen.

Eastman Kodak Co., *Kodak Pocket Photoguide*, Tiffen.

Frost, Lee, *The Question-and-Answer Guide to Photo Techniques*, David & Charles.

Grimm, Tom and Michele, *The Basic Book of Photography*, 4th ed., Plume.

Hedgecoe, John, *The Art of Colour Photography*, Butterwork-Heinemann.

Hedgecoe, John, *John Hedgecoe's Complete Guide to Photography*, Sterling.

Hedgecoe, John, *John Hedgecoe's Photography Basics*, Sterling.

Hedgecoe, John, *The Photographer's Handbook*, Alfred A. Knopf.

Kodak, *How to Take Good Pictures*, Ballantine.

London, Barbara (Editor), and John Upton (Contributor), *Photography*, Addison-Watson-Guptill.

Peterson, Bryan, *Learning to See Creatively*, Amphoto.

Peterson, Bryan, *Understanding Exposure*, Amphoto.

Equipment-Oriented Books

Burian, Peter K. (Editor), *Camera Basics*, Eastman Kodak, Silver Pixel Press.

Eastman Kodak Co., *Using Filters*, Tiffen.

Meehan, Joseph, *The Complete Book of Photographic Lenses*, Amphoto.

Meehan, Joseph, *Panoramic Photography*, Revised Edition, Watson-Guptill.

Meehan, Joseph, *The Photographer's Guide to Using Filters*, Watson-Guptill.

Neubart, Jack, *Electronic Flash*, Tiffen.

Simmons, Steve, *Using the View Camera*, Amphoto.

Outdoor and Nature Photography Books

Benvie, Niall, *The Art of Nature Photography*, Watson-Guptill.

Caulfield, Patricia, *Capturing the Landscape with Your Camera*, Watson-Guptill.

Fielder, John, *Photographing the Landscape*, Westcliffe.

Fitzharris, Tim, *The Sierra Club Guide to Close-up Photography in Nature*, Sierra Club Books.

Hedgecoe, John, *Photographing Landscapes*, Collins & Brown.

Lange, Joseph K., *How to Photograph Landscapes*, Stackpole Books.

Lloyd, Harvey, *Aerial Photography*, Watson-Guptill.

Nichols, Clive, *Photographing Plants and Gardens*, David & Charles.

Norton, Boyd, *The Art of Outdoor Photography*, Voyageur Press.

Rokach, Alan and Anne Millman, *Field Guide to Photographing Flowers*, Amphoto.

Rokach, Alan and Anne Millman, *Field Guide to Photographing Gardens*, Watson-Guptill.

Rokach, Alan and Anne Millman, *Field Guide to Photographing Landscapes*. Amphoto.

Rotenberg, Nancy and Michael Lustbader, *How to Photograph Close-Ups in Nature*, Stackpole.

Shaw, John, *John Shaw's Landscape Photography*, Amphoto.

Shaw, John, *John Shaw's Nature Photography Field Guide*, Amphoto.

Travel Photography Books

Eastman Kodak Co., *Kodak Pocket Guide to Travel Photography*, Hungry Minds.

Frost, Lee, *The Complete Guide to Night and Low Light Photography*, Watson-Guptill.

Krist, Bob, *Spirit of Place: The Art of the Traveling Photographer*, Amphoto.

McCartney, Susan, *Travel Photography*, Second Edition, Allworth Press.

Wignall, Jeff, *Kodak Guide to Shooting Great Travel Pictures*, Fodor's Travel Publications.

Robert Caputo, coauthor of the *National Geographic Photography Field Guide*, has been photographing and writing stories for the *National Geographic Society* since 1980. His award-winning work has also appeared in numerous other magazines and has been included in international exhibitions. Publisher of two children's wildlife books and two photo-essay books, *Journey up the Nile* and *Kenya Journey*, Caputo appeared in and wrote the narration for the *National Geographic Explorer* film *Zaire River Journey* and wrote the story for and was associate producer of *Glory & Honor*, the TNT original film about the discovery of the North Pole. He lives in Pennsylvania.

Index

A

ACDSee Photo Manager 348
Action photography
  aperture 79
  camera settings 67–68
  flash blur 126
  freezing 120–122
  sensor sensitivity 79
  shutter delay 186
  shutter priority 67–68
  shutter speed 79
Adams, Ansel 191, 301
Adamson, Robert 277
Adobe
  Digital Negative format (DNG) 353
Adobe Bridge 350
Adobe Gamma 330
Adobe Photoshop 220–249
  Auto Color 234
  Auto Levels 226
  brightness adjustment 224–225,
    226–227, 230–232
  burning 245–247
  Camera Raw plug-in 222
  color balance 232–235, 237–238
  contrast adjustment 225, 226–228
  converting color to black-and-white
    248
  cropping 242–244
  Curves adjustment 230–232
  dodging 245–247
  Exposure 223–224
  filters 247–248
  Gaussian Blur 240, 241–242
  highlight adjustment 229, 230–232
  history 308–309
  hue/saturation adjustment 237–238,
    248
  layers 247
  Levels 229–230, 234
  monitor calibration wizard 264
  red-eye elimination 25
  scanning 333, 334–335
  shadow adjustment 224, 229–232,
    235
  sharpness adjustment 238–241
  tone adjustment 225–232, 248
  Unsharp Mask tool 239–241
Adobe Photoshop CS 336
Adobe Photoshop CS2 350, 372
Adobe Photoshop Elements 264, 347
Albumen process 278–279
Allard, William Albert
  portfolio 310–317
Allen, Steve 306
The Americans (Frank) 180, 185, 202, 204,
  303
Anderson, Christopher 34
Angle finder 127
Angles of view
  fisheye lenses 57
  photography of children 158
  standard lens 51
  wide-angle lens 52
Aperture
  definition 16
  and depth of field 79, 82
  environmental portraits 132–133
  full-length portraits 132
  macro photography 168
  still life photography 164
  tips 66

wildlife photography 154
  and zoom lenses 56
Aperture priority setting 16, 67
Apple Aperture 350
Arago, François 276
Archer, Frederick Scott 279
Archiving
  on CD-Roms 31–32, 345–346, 349,
    350–351, 353–355
  deleting photographs 348–349
  on DVDs 350–351, 353–354
  file naming 345, 348
  file types 352–353
  minimalist approach 344–346
  off-site storage 351
  photo albums 374–375
  rating photographs 348
  software 346–347, 348, 350, 355
  storage options 350–351
  worst-case scenarios 352–356
Art photography 302–303
Atkins, Anna 275
Auto-bracket setting 70
Auto-focus 76–79
Auto white balance (AWB) 90, 91, 222
Autochromes 290
Automobile photography
  tracking 124

B

"Back button focusing" 78
Backgrounds
  black 99
  environmental portraits 132–133
  full-length portraits 132
  importance 93–95
  photography of children 159
  in portraits 141
  still life photography 161–164
Bale, Kevin 108
Ballmer, Steve 306
Banks, Dennis 298
Barnack, Oscar 291, 294
Barnard, George N. 283, 285
Battery life 48, 59
Bellows 168
Belt, Annie Griffiths
  portfolio 358–359
Bischof, Werner 300
Bissinger, Buzz 201
Black-and-white photography
  cameraphone 182–183, 185–186, 195,
    205
  longevity of prints 255
  low light images 298
  reasons for 205
  software conversion from color 103,
    248, 249
Blackmon, Julie
  portfolio 250–251
Blanquart-Evrard, Louis Désiré 278
Blurring
  flash blur 125–126
  movement blur 124–125
  night photography 147–148
  panning 122–123
  in Photoshop 241–242
  shutter speed 124–125
Bounce flash 98–99
Bourke-White, Margaret 296
Bracketing 70
Brightness
  adjusting in Photoshop 224–225,
    226–227, 230–232
Brodovitch, Alexey 302–303
Burnett, David 292–293
Burning (technique)

in Photoshop 245–247
Burrows, Chet 201–202
Burrows, Larry 298
BW Workflow Pro 246, 248

C

Cakes, photo 364–365
Calendars 366–367
Calotypes 277
Camera Bits PhotoMechanic 350
Camera lucida 276
Camera obscura 272, 309
Cameraless photography 275
Cameraphone photography 180–208
  black-and-white 182–183, 185–186,
    205
  color 182–183, 185–186
  composition 186, 197
  depth of field 182
  exposure 200
  lighting 185–186
  tips 182, 185, 194, 204
  zoom lens 194
Cameras
  invention 272–274
Cameron, Julia Margaret 283
Capa, Robert 296–298, 300
Card readers 32
Carroll, Lewis 279
Cartier-Bresson, Henri 291
CCD (Charge Coupled Device) 15, 48, 59
CD-Roms
  archiving 31–32, 345–346, 349,
    350–351, 353–355
  labeling 261, 354–355
  longevity 309, 353–354
  reliability 353–354
Cellular phones *see* Cameraphone photography
Center-weighted metering 71
Charge Coupled Device (CCD) 15, 48, 59
Children
  photography of 155, 158–160
Civil War, U.S.
  photographs 278, 285
Clark, Dora Lou 191
Clark, Robert
  cameraphone photography 180–187,
    190–207
Clark, Russell 191
Close, Chuck 309
Close-up photography
  attachments 167
  lenses 56–57
  lighting 130–131
  perspective distortion 132
  wildlife photography 155
  see also Macro photography
CMOS 15–16, 48
Cobb, Jodi
  portfolio 108–117
Color
  balance 59, 90–91, 232–235, 237–238
  and composition 87
  hue and saturation adjustment
    237–238
  monitor calibration 219–220,
    264–265, 329–330
  temperature 222–223
Comic Life 362, 363
Comicbook Creator 362
Comics 362–363
Complementary Metal Oxide
    Semiconductor (CMOS)
    15–16, 48
Composition
  backgrounds 93–95

basic rules 82–87
  color 87
  cropping 242
  group portraits 133
  lines 87
  night photography 146
  perspective 86–87
  rule of thirds 86
  still lifes 164
  tips 18, 85
  viewpoints 86–87
Computer monitors
  calibration 219–220, 264–265,
    329–330
  color and tone 218–219
Contrast
  adjusting in Photoshop 225, 226–228
Corel Album 348
Coventry, David 203, 204
Cropping
  in Photoshop 242–244
CRT monitor screens 330
Cyanotype process 275

D

D-SLR cameras
  auto-bracket setting 70
  buying tips 10–11, 48
  checklist 59
  description 10
  Exposure Compensation setting
    66–70
  lenses 50–53, 56–58, 62
  metering modes 70–71, 75
  sensors 48–49
  software 48
  types 46–47
Daguerre, Louis-Jacques-Mandé 274,
  276–277
Daguerreotypes 276, 277, 309
Depth of field
  and aperture 79, 82
  cameraphone photography 182
  definition 79
  and focal length 79
  macro photography 166, 168
  still life photography 164
  telephoto lenses 53, 79, 82
  wide-angle lenses 79, 82
  wildlife photography 154, 155
Derges, Susan 275
Digital cameras
  auto white balance (AWB) 90
  buying tips 8–11, 48
  disadvantages 128
  history 150, 307–309
  noise 143, 146
  point and shoot 8–9
  sensors 15–16
  software updates 48
  see also D-SLR
Digital Negative format (DNG) 353
Digital single lens reflex cameras see D-
  SLR cameras
Digitizing images see Scanning
Disuvero, Alex 204
DNG (Digital Negative format) 353
Documentary photography
  Depression era 295–296
  weddings 148, 149, 153
Dodging (editing technique) 245–247
Driffield, Vero Charles 279–280
DVDs
  archiving 350–351, 353–354
  longevity 309, 353–354
  reliability 353–354

E

Eastman, George 282

Eastman Kodak Company
  cameras 282, 303, 306
  film 294–295, 310
  slogan 282
Edge contrast 239
Edison, Thomas Alva 291
Editing software 27–28
  see also Adobe Photoshop; iPhoto
Ektachrome film 295
Emerson, Peter Henry 287
Engelbart, Douglas 307
Environmental portraits 132–133
Eppridge, Bill 298
Evans, Walker 296, 303
EXIF format 9, 355
Exposure
  adjusting in Photoshop 223–224
  automatic 65, 67, 218
  basic rules 62–64, 216–218
  cameraphone photography 200
  compensation 66–70
  controlling light 64–66
  definition 15, 62
  manual 70
  metering modes 70–71, 75
  night photography 146
  override facility 18
  photography of children 159
  point-and-shoot cameras 15–16, 18
  sensor sensitivity 65
  and shutter speed 99–100
  see also Histograms
Extension tubes 167
Extensis Portfolio 350

F

F-stops
  definition 62
  macro photography 168
  setting 16
  tips 66
  zoom lenses 56
Farber, Chris 193
Farm Security Administration (FSA)
  295–296
Fenton, Roger 284–285
File formats
  JPEG 48, 59, 64, 92, 309, 350, 352
  obsolescence 352–353
  overview 92
  RAW 48, 59, 64, 92, 350, 353
  TIFF 59, 92
Fill flash 25, 102–103, 136, 148–149
Filters
  digital 247–248
Firmware
  updating 48
Fisheye lenses 57
Flash photography
  basic rules 95, 98–99
  with blur 125–126
  bounce flash 98–99
  built-in flash 95, 98
  coloured gel 101
  diffusion 99
  fill flash 25, 102–103, 136, 148–149
  macro photography 166, 168–169
  night photography 146
  point-and-shoot cameras 20, 24
  portable flashes 100–102
  ring flash 166
  shadows 98
  slave unit 101
  studio portraits 136–137, 140
  sync plugs 101
  sync speed 102
  synchronization 126
  tips 101

weddings 148–149
Focal length
  and depth of field 79
  and macro lenses 56
  night photography 148
  and perspective 62
  photography of children 158–159
  point-and-shoot cameras 19
  and sensor size 50
  telephoto lenses 53
Focus
  focus lock facility 20
  macro photography 168
  manual 78–79
  still life photography 164
Focusing stage 168
Framing (composition) 82–87
Frank, Robert 180, 185, 204, 302–303
Freezing motion 120–122
Fuss, Adam 275, 309

G

Gardner, Alexander 285
Garrett, Kenneth 72–73
Gates, Bill 306
Gaussian Blur 241–242
Green, Evan 194–195
Greeting cards 376–377
Group portraits 52, 133
Guariglia, Justin 60–61

H

Halftone photographs 285–286
Hand-held metering 71, 75
Hare, Jimmy 286
Hawass, Zahi 72
Hearst, William Randolph 291
Heliography 273–274
Herschel, Sir John 277, 282
Hickey, Eamon 34
Highlights
  adjusting in Photoshop 229, 230–232
Hill, David Octavius 277
Histograms 63, 75–76, 326–327, 335
Holga cameras 292
Hurter, Ferdinand 279–280

I

ICC profile 265
Imacon scanner 328
Image America (Clark) 180
iPhoto 27–28, 267, 346–347
IPTC data 355
Iron-on transfers 378–379
ISO (sensor sensitivity) 16, 49, 59, 65, 79
IView Media Pro 350

J

Jobs, Steve 307
JPEG file format 48, 59, 64, 92, 309, 350,
  352

K

Kaye, Russell 301
Kleinrock, Leonard 307
Knoll, John 308–309
Knoll, Thomas 308–309
Kodachrome 294–295, 310
Kodacolor film 295
Kodak see Eastman Kodak Company
Koudelka, Josef 300

L

Laforet, Bertrand 150
Laforet, Vincent 150–151
Laman, Tim 138–139
Land, Edwin H. 300, 302
Landscape photography
  aperture 79
  composition 86, 203
  depth of field 79
  lenses 52, 53
  panoramas 370–371

and time of day 107
tips 82, 107
Lange, Dorothea 295–296
LCD monitor screens 330
Le Gray, Gustave 278–279, 283
Lee, Russell 296
Lenses
fixed focal-length 56
focal length 19, 50
general-purpose 51
macro 56–57, 155, 167
macro photography 166, 167–168
and perspective 62
photography of children 158
shift 57–58
split field 58
standard lenses 50, 51, 62
still life photography 164
telephoto (*see* Telephoto lenses)
types 50
wide-angle (*see* Wide-angle lenses)
zoom (*see* Zoom lenses)
Life magazine 296, 297–298
Lighting
aperture priority 67
cameraphone photography 185–186
close-up portraits 130–131
metering 70–71, 75
photography of children 159
portraits 133, 136, 141
reflectors 136
sense of depth 87
sensor sensitivity 49
still life photography 160–161, 162, 163–164
studio 136–137, 140
time of day 103, 106–107, 136, 185, 197–199
tungsten 136–137
Ling, Lai 195–202
Lumière, Auguste 290
Lumière, Louis 290

M

Macintosh computers
calibration 264
see also iPhoto
Macro lenses 56–57, 155, 167
Macro photography 165–169
Maddox, Richard 279
Magnum (photo agency) 298, 300
portfolio 34–43
Majoli, Alex 34
Mann, Sally 309
McCombe, Leonard 298
Memory buffer 48
Memory cards 9, 31, 32, 48, 59
Metadata 350, 355
Miranda, Fred 246, 248
Moholy-Nagy, Laszlo 275
Moonen, Rick 195–196
Morell, Abelardo 309
Morris, John 297–298
Motion
freezing 120–122
movement blur 124–125
panning 122–124
photography of children 159
tracking 124
see also Action photography
Movement blur 124–125
Mutchler, Kurt 203

N

Negatives
cleaning 332
scanning 332–333, 335, 356
News photography 283–286, 290–291
Nichols, Michael "Nick"

portfolio 170–177
Niépce, Isidore 276
Niépce, Joseph Nicéphore 272–274
Night photography 142–143, 146–148
Nik Color Efex filters 248
Nikon Coolscan 329
Nikon FM2 128
Noise 143, 146

O

Olson, Randy
portfolio 268–269
"One-shot" focusing 76–78
Optical zoom lenses 8, 19

P

Panning 122–123
Panoramas 370–371
Parks, Gordon 296
Pellegrin, Paolo 34–35
Perspective 58, 62, 86–87, 132
Photo albums 374–375
Photo (computer program) 348
Photo Secessionists 287, 290
Photogenic drawings 275
Photograms 275, 309
Photography
cameraless 275
history 272–274, 276–280
Photojournalism 285–286
Photoshop *see* Adobe Photoshop
Picasa 348
PictBridge 258
Pictorialism 287
Pinhole cameras 288–289
Point-and-shoot cameras
aperture priority 16
automatic settings 16
automatic settings override 16, 18, 20
basic advice 14–26
buying tips 8–9
description 8
exposure 15–16, 18
flash use 20, 24
focusing 18
photo composition 18
professional use 34
red-eye reduction mode 25
shutter speed priority 16
zooming 18
Polaroid cameras 300, 302
Pop art 368–369
Pope, Wes 288–289
Portraits
backgrounds 141
close-ups 130–132
composition 85–86, 86–87
flash photography 136–137, 140
full-length 132
lenses for 56
lighting 130–131, 133, 136, 141
many-faces poster 372–373
pop art 368–369
studio 136–137, 140
and time of day 107, 136
tips 107, 141–142
types 130
wedding 148–149
wildlife 154
Posters
many faces 372–373
Printers
all-in-one 258
buying tips 256, 259, 261–262
connectivity 259
dedicated photoprinters 30, 256–257, 258
driver software 265
dye-sublimation 258

inkjet 30, 257–258, 355–356
inks 259–261
paper capacity 259, 261–262
resolution 266–267
settings 265
types 29–30, 256–258
Printing
on canvas 369
costs 262
ICC profile 265
outsourcing 27, 30–31, 267, 363, 369
paper choices 30
photo cakes 364
tips 30, 256, 264, 267
Program exposure mode 67, 69–70
Projects
calendars 366–367
comics 362–363
greeting cards 376–377
many faces poster 372–373
panoramas 370–371
photo albums 374–375
photo cakes 364–365
photo transfers 378–379
pop-art prints 368–369

R

RAW file format 48, 59, 64, 92, 220–222, 350, 353
Ray, Man 275
Rayographs 275
Rear-curtain synchronization 126
Red-eye effect 25, 140
Rejlander, Oscar 283
Remote cameras 126–127, 130
Reverse lens adaptor 168
Right angle prism viewfinder 167
Riis, Jacob 285
Ring flash 166
Robinson, Henry Peach 283
Rothstein, Arthur 296
Rotogravure 286

S

Salgado, Sebastiao 300
Scanners
bit depth 325
bulk-scanner attachment 329
description 320–321
dynamic range 326, 328–329
features 324–327, 329
film 320, 327–328
flatbed 320–321, 328–329, 333
histograms 326–327, 335
resolution 324–325
selection 323–327
types 320–321, 327–329
uses 320, 322
Scanning
Auto Adjustments 333
dust removal 333–335
monitor calibration 329–330
negatives 332–333, 335
outsourcing 335, 356–357
preview 333
prints 333
procedures 331–335
software 333
tips 335
Schulze, Johann Heinrich 272
Second-curtain synchronization 126
Sensors
buying tips 48–49
cleaning 59
description 15–16
and focal length 50
full-frame 154
sensitivity 16, 49, 59, 65, 79
size 49

tips 154
types 48
Seymour, David 300
Shadows
adjusting in Photoshop 224, 229–232, 235
Shahn, Ben 296
Sharpness
adjusting in Photoshop 238–241
Shepherd, Cybil 303
Shift lenses 57–58
Shutter delay 48, 150, 186
Shutter priority mode 16, 67–68
Shutter speed
action photography 124
blur 123, 124–125
definition 16, 62–63
experimentation 170–171
and exposure 99–100
flash blur 125–126
freezing motion 120–122
macro photography 168
night photography 143, 146
noise 143, 146
panning 123
photography of children 159
still life photography 164
tips 66
tracking 124
wildlife photography 154
Silhouettes 136
Single lens reflex cameras (SLR) 306
see also D-SLR
"Single servo" focusing 76–78
Slide shows 28–29
Slides
digitizing 322, 356
film 295
Smith, W. Eugene 298
Soda can cameras 288–289
Sony Ericsson cameraphone 180
Speed Graphic camera 290–291, 292
Split field lenses 58
Sports photography 53
see also Action photography
Spot metering 71
St.-Victor, Claude Félix Abel Niépce de 278
Steinbeck, John 185
Stereo cards 280–282
Sternberg, Max 182, 185, 193
Stieglitz, Alfred 287, 290
Still life photography 160–165
Stout, D. J. 202
Stryker, Roy E. 295, 296
Synchro sun see Fill flash
T
Talbot, William Henry Fox 275, 276–277
Talbotypes see Calotypes
Taylor, Joe 201
Taylor, Maggie
portfolio 336–337
Teleconverters 58
Telephoto lenses
depth of field 53, 79, 82
focal length 50, 53
landscape photography 53
and perspective 62
photography of children 158
portraits 56
and sensor size 49
still life photography 164
uses 52–53, 56, 94
wedding photography 149
35mm cameras 291, 294, 306
TIFF file format 59, 92
Tomaszewski, Tomasz 181

Tonality
adjusting in Photoshop 225–232, 248
Tracking 124
Tripods 160, 166, 168
Tungsten light 136–137
V
Viewfinders
right angle prism 167
Vision
color balancing 214–215
depth 87
W
Ward, Larry 204–205
Warhol, Andy 368
Wedding photography 148–149, 153
Wedgwood family 272
Wet collodion process 279, 309
Wide-angle lenses
depth of field 79, 82
environmental portraits 133
fisheye lenses 57
focal length 50
group portraits 52
landscape photography 52

and perspective 62
sense of depth 87
and sensor size 49
uses 51–52
Wildlife photography 153–155, 170
Wiltsie, Gordon 128–129
World War II
photography 296–298
Wozniak, Steve 307
Z
Zoom lenses
aperture 56
cameraphones 194
and composition 85
digital zoom 8, 194
macro photography 167–168
night photography 148
optical zoom 8, 19
uses 19
wedding photography 149

Photo Credits

COVER: Anup and Manoj Shah.

FRONT MATTER: 2-3, Jodi Cobb, NGS; 4, Andreas Feininger/Time Life Pictures/Getty Images; 7, Macduff Everton.

CHAPTER 1, THE LANDSCAPE PHOTOGRAPH: 8-9, Jim Richardson; 10, Sam Abell; 11, Carsten Peter/NGS Image Collection; 13, Maria Stenzel; 14, Tim Laman; 15, Otis Imboden; 16-17, Michael Melford; 19, Jim Richardson; 20, James P. Blair; 22-23, Raymond Gehman/NGS Image Collection; 25, Chris Johns, NGS; 26-27, Peter Essick; 28-29, Jim Richardson; 30-31, Joel Sartore; 33, Sam Abell; 34-41, Raymond Gehman.

CHAPTER 2, COMPOSITION: 42-43, Sam Abell; 44, Michael Melford; 45, Jodi Cobb, NGS; 47, Robert Caputo; 48-49, Sam Abell; 51, Charles Kogod; 52-53, Sarah Leen; 54, Mattias Klum/NGS Image Collection; 55, Sarah Leen; 56-57, Bruce Dale; 58, Robb Kendrick; 59, Annie Griffiths Belt; 60-61, Library of Congress, Prints & Photographs Division (#LC-DIG-fsac-1a33901); 63, Jodi Cobb, NGS; 64, Robert Caputo; 65, George Steinmetz; 66-67, Robert Caputo; 68-77, Joel Sartore.

CHAPTER 3, USING LIGHT EFFECTIVELY: 78-79, Macduff Everton; 80, Sam Abell; 81, Ira Block/NGS Image Collection; 82-83, Ian C. Martin; 84, Jim Richardson; 85, Sam Abell; 86-90, Robert Caputo; 92-93, Michael Melford; 94, Susie Post Rust; 96-97, Sisse Brimberg; 99, Sam Abell; 100, William Albert Allard, NGS; 102-103, Joel Sartore; 104, Frans Lanting; 106-107, Bruce Dale; 109, Mark Thiessen, NGS; 110-111, Joanna B. Pinneo; 113-119, Bruce Dale.

CHAPTER 4, CAMERAS & LENSES: 120-121, George Steinmetz; 122 & 123, Gordon Wiltsie; 124, John Shaw/Panoramic Images, Chicago; 127, Robert Caputo; 128-129, Gerd Ludwig; 131, Chuck Kirman/Ventura County Star/CORBIS; 132, Robert Caputo; 134-135, Justin Guariglia/NGS Image Collection; 137, Macduff Everton.

CHAPTER 5, DIGITAL STRATEGIES: 138-139, Michael Melford; 140, Jay Dickman; 141, Michael Nichols/NGS Image Collection; 142, Richard Olsenius; 143, John Healey; 144 & 145 (upper), Mark Thiessen, NGS; 146-150, Robert Caputo.

THE ULTIMATE FIELD GUIDE TO LANDSCAPE PHOTOGRAPHY

ROBERT CAPUTO

Published by the National Geographic Society

John M. Fahey, Jr., President and
Chief Executive Officer

Gilbert M. Grosvenor, Chairman of the Board

Nina D. Hoffman, Executive Vice President;
President, Books PublishingGroup

Prepared by the Book Division

Kevin Mulroy, Senior Vice President and Publisher

Leah Bendavid-Val, Director of Photography
Publishing and Illustrations

Marianne R. Koszorus, Director of Design

Barbara Brownell Grogan, Executive Editor

Elizabeth Newhouse, Director of Travel Publishing

Carl Mehler, Director of Maps

Staff for this Book

Bronwen Latimer, Editor and Illustrations Editor

Peggy Archambault, Art Director

Rebecca Barns, Text Editor

Mike Horenstein, Production Project Manager

Meredith C. Wilcox, Illustrations Specialist

Allison Morrow, Design Intern

Rebecca Hinds, Managing Editor

Gary Colbert, Production Director

Manufacturing and Quality Management

Christopher A. Liedel, Chief Financial Officer

Phillip L. Schlosser, Vice President

John T. Dunn, Technical Director

Vincent P. Ryan, Director

Chris Brown, Director

Maryclare Tracy, Manager

Founded in 1888, the National Geographic Society is one of the largest nonprofit scientific and educational organizations in the world.

It reaches more than 285 million people worldwide each month through its official journal, NATIONAL GEOGRAPHIC, and its four other magazines; the National Geographic Channel; television documentaries; radio programs; films; books; videos and DVDs; maps; and interactive media. National Geographic has funded more than 8,000 scientific research projects and supports an education program combating geographic illiteracy.

For more information, please call
1-800-NGS LINE (647-5463)
or write to the following address:

National Geographic Society
1145 17th Street N.W.
Washington, D.C. 20036-4688 U.S.A.

Visit us online at
www.nationalgeographic.com/books

For information about special discounts
for bulk purchases, please contact
National Geographic Books Special Sales:
ngspecsales@ngs.org

Library of Congress Cataloging-in-Publication Data
available upon request

ISBN: 978-1-4262-0054-0

Printed in Spain